「目で見る児童福祉2021」目次
"Graphs and Charts on Japan's Child Welfare Services 2021"
Table of Contents

JN093294

目で見る児童福祉

Graphs and Charts on Japan's Child Welfare Services

2021

公益財団法人 **児童育成協会**
The Foundation for Child Well-being

【本書の内容現在】【Contents of this document】

本書に収載されている統計数値は、2021年2月25日までに公表されたデータをもとに更新しました。各制度においても同様に更新しました。

The statistics in this book have been updated based on data published by February 25, 2021. Systems have been similarly updated.

児童福祉の理念と課題
The Basic Idea and the Task of Japan's Child Welfare Services

児童福祉法［法令番号:昭和22年法律第164号］
Child welfare Act［law number:Act No.164 of 1947］

児童の福祉を保障するための原理 Principles to Guarantee Welfare of Children

第一条 全て児童は、児童の権利に関する条約の精神にのつとり、適切に養育されること、その生活を保障されること、愛され、保護されること、その心身の健やかな成長及び発達並びにその自立が図られることその他の福祉を等しく保障される権利を有する。

Article 1 Based on the spirit of the Convention on the Rights of the Child, all children shall have the right to be properly cared for, guaranteed for such life, loved, protected, nurtured for their healthy physical/mental growth/development and independence, as well as equally guaranteed for other aspects of welfare.

児童育成の責任 Responsibility for the Healthy Growth of Children

第二条 全て国民は、児童が良好な環境において生まれ、かつ、社会のあらゆる分野において、児童の年齢及び発達の程度に応じて、その意見が尊重され、その最善の利益が優先して考慮され、心身ともに健やかに育成されるよう努めなければならない。
② 児童の保護者は、児童を心身ともに健やかに育成することについて第一義的責任を負う。
③ 国及び地方公共団体は、児童の保護者とともに、児童を心身ともに健やかに育成する責任を負う。

Article 2 All citizens shall endeavor to ensure that children are born in a good environment, have their opinions respected in every field in a society in accordance with their age and developmental stage, have their best interest prioritized, and are brought up in good mental and physical health.
(2) Guardians have the primary responsibility for bringing up children in good mental and physical health.
(3) The national and local governments shall be responsible for bringing up children in good mental and physical health, along with their guardians.

原理の尊重 Respect for the Principles of Child Welfare

第三条 前二条に規定するところは、児童の福祉を保障するための原理であり、この原理は、すべて児童に関する法令の施行にあたつて、常に尊重されなければならない。

Article 3 The provisions of the preceding two Articles constitute the basic philosophy to guarantee children's welfare and this philosophy shall be consistently respected in enforcing all laws and regulations on children.

　我が国の児童福祉施策は、昭和22年（1947年）に公布された児童福祉法を基本とし、関連する各種法律に基づいて推進されている。
　平均寿命の伸長、出生率の低下等に伴い少子高齢社会を迎えている今日、次代の社会を担う児童を心身ともに健全に育成することは、緊急かつ重要な国民的課題となっている。
　この課題を達成するため、保護者とともに、国、地方公共団体は相互に連携をとりながら児童福祉の向上に努めている。

Child welfare services in Japan have been carried out on the basis of the Child Welfare Law, enacted in 1947, and other related laws.
Considering that Japan's population is rapidly aging due to the facts such as the growth of the average life span and the recent decline of the birth rate, it is an urgent and important national task to rear physically and mentally healthy children who will shoulder the coming ages.
In order to accomplish this task, the central and prefectural governments together with individual parents are working in cooperation to improve the quality of child welfare.

児童家庭福祉施策の全体像 An Overview of Measures for Children and Family Welfare

子どもの成長過程に応じた各施策
Measures according to the child's growth process

妊娠期
Pregnancy period

出産
Childbearing

乳・幼児期
Nursing infant period

就学児童
School-age child

18歳
18 years old

20歳
20 years old

母子保健 Mother and Child Health

・母子健康手帳
Maternal and child health handbook

・妊婦健診
Medical checkups for pregnant women

乳児健診
Health checkups for infants

新生児訪問
Home visit to newborns

乳・幼児健診
Health checkups for infants

地域子育て支援拠点
Community-based childrearing support center

保育所
Day-care center

幼保連携型認定こども園
Center for early childhood education and care (integrated center model)

児童館・児童センター
Children's hall・Children's center

放課後児童クラブ
After-school children's club

各時期共通
Each time commonness

虐待防止
Abuse prevention

ひとり親家庭
Single-parent home

障害児
Disabled children

社会的養護
Social care service

家庭の状況に応じた相談機関等
consultant facilities according to situation of family , etc

多い many

少ない few

児童家庭センター
Children and families supporting center

市町村 Municipalities

・子ども家庭総合支援拠点
Comprehensive support center for children and families

・家庭児童相談室
Family and children's guidance room

・要保護児童対策地域協議会
Regional council for children in need of protection

ハイリスク家庭
High-risk families

一般子育て家庭
Childcare families

・市町村保健センター
Health centers

・NPOなど民間団体
Non-governmental organization

保健所
Health center

社会的養護 Social care service

里親・ファミリーホーム Foster parent・Family home

児童養護施設 Children's home

児童心理治療施設
Psychological treatment facilities for children

児童自立支援施設
Support facilities for development of self-sustaining capacity

母子生活支援施設
Daily life support facilities for mothers and children

在宅支援家庭
Families receiving in-home support

家庭分離・子どもの保護（社会的養護）
Separating family members Protection of children (Social care service)

児童委員
Commissioned child welfare volunteer

児童相談所
Child guidance center

軽度 mild

重度 severe

年齢別児童家庭福祉施策の一覧 Age-specific Service Programs for the Child and Family Welfare

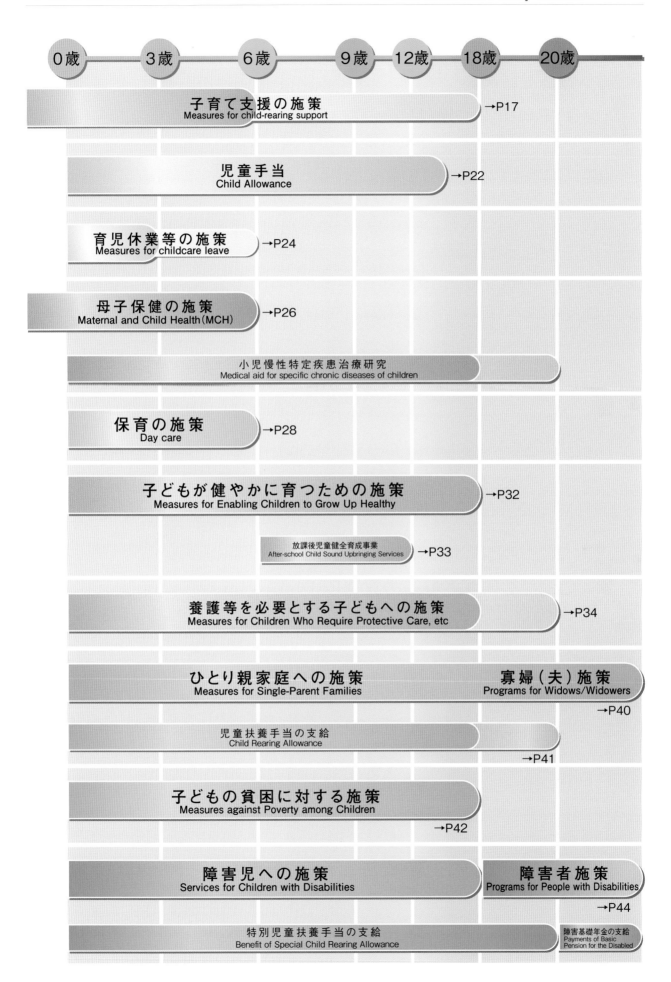

| 0歳 | 3歳 | 6歳 | 9歳 | 12歳 | 18歳 | 20歳 |

子育て支援の施策
Measures for child-rearing support →P17

児童手当
Child Allowance →P22

育児休業等の施策
Measures for childcare leave →P24

母子保健の施策
Maternal and Child Health（MCH） →P26

小児慢性特定疾患治療研究
Medical aid for specific chronic diseases of children

保育の施策
Day care →P28

子どもが健やかに育つための施策
Measures for Enabling Children to Grow Up Healthy →P32

放課後児童健全育成事業
After-school Child Sound Upbringing Services →P33

養護等を必要とする子どもへの施策
Measures for Children Who Require Protective Care, etc →P34

ひとり親家庭への施策
Measures for Single-Parent Families

寡婦（夫）施策
Programs for Widows/Widowers →P40

児童扶養手当の支給
Child Rearing Allowance →P41

子どもの貧困に対する施策
Measures against Poverty among Children →P42

障害児への施策
Services for Children with Disabilities

障害者施策
Programs for People with Disabilities →P44

特別児童扶養手当の支給
Benefit of Special Child Rearing Allowance

障害基礎年金の支給
Payments of Basic Pension for the Disabled

1. 総　論
General Remarks

(1)人口動向 Population Trends

1 2019年の人口構成
Population Pyramid in 2019

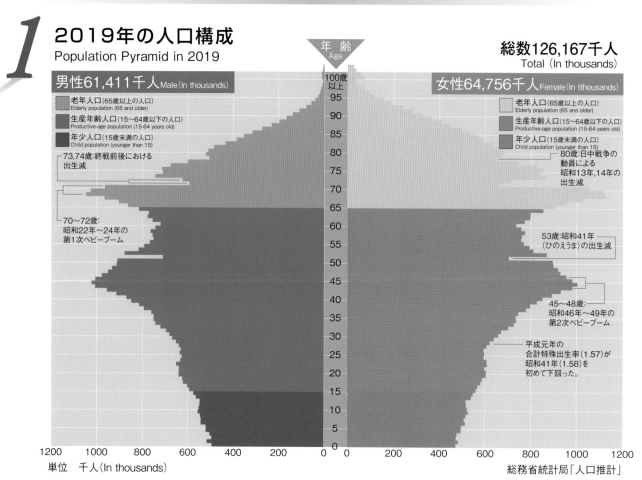

男性61,411千人Male(In thousands)

- 老年人口(65歳以上の人口) Elderly population (65 and older)
- 生産年齢人口(15～64歳以下の人口) Productive-age population (15-64 years old)
- 年少人口(15歳未満の人口) Child population (younger than 15)

年 齢 Age
100歳以上

- 73,74歳:終戦前後における出生減
- 70～72歳: 昭和22年～24年の第1次ベビーブーム

総数126,167千人
Total (In thousands)

女性64,756千人Female(In tthousands)

- 老年人口(65歳以上の人口) Elderly population (65 and older)
- 生産年齢人口(15～64歳以下の人口) Productive-age population (15-64 years old)
- 年少人口(15歳未満の人口) Child population (younger than 15)

- 80歳:日中戦争の動員による昭和13年,14年の出生減
- 53歳:昭和41年(ひのえうま)の出生減
- 45～48歳:昭和46年～49年の第2次ベビーブーム
- 平成元年の合計特殊出生率(1.57)が昭和41年(1.58)を初めて下回った。

単位　千人(In thousands)

総務省統計局「人口推計」

2 人口構成の推移と将来の見通し
Trends in Population Composition and Outlook of Future Population

年齢別人口および推計年齢別将来人口
Population by age and outlook of future population by age

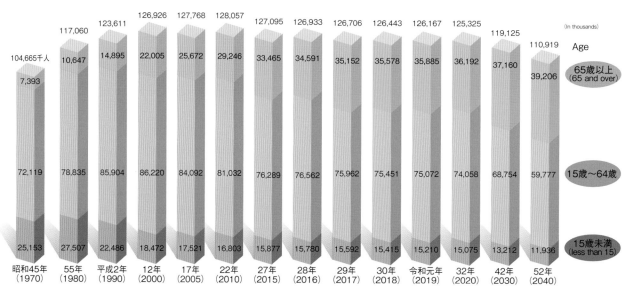

(In thousands)

Age

	昭和45年(1970)	55年(1980)	平成2年(1990)	12年(2000)	17年(2005)	22年(2010)	27年(2015)	28年(2016)	29年(2017)	30年(2018)	令和元年(2019)	32年(2020)	42年(2030)	52年(2040)
総数	104,665千人	117,060	123,611	126,926	127,768	128,057	127,095	126,933	126,706	126,443	126,167	125,325	119,125	110,919
65歳以上 (65 and over)	7,393	10,647	14,895	22,005	25,672	29,246	33,465	34,591	35,152	35,578	35,885	36,192	37,160	39,206
15歳～64歳	72,119	78,835	85,904	86,220	84,092	81,032	76,289	76,562	75,962	75,451	75,072	74,058	68,754	59,777
15歳未満 (less than 15)	25,153	27,507	22,486	18,472	17,521	16,803	15,877	15,780	15,592	15,415	15,210	15,075	13,212	11,936

(～平成27年)総務省統計局「国勢調査」
(平成28年～令和元年)総務省統計局人口推計(各年10月1日現在)
(平成32年～)国立社会保障・人口問題研究所「日本の将来推計人口(平成29年4月推計)」

3 出生の動向
Trends in Total Fertility Rate, Number of Live Births and Birthrate

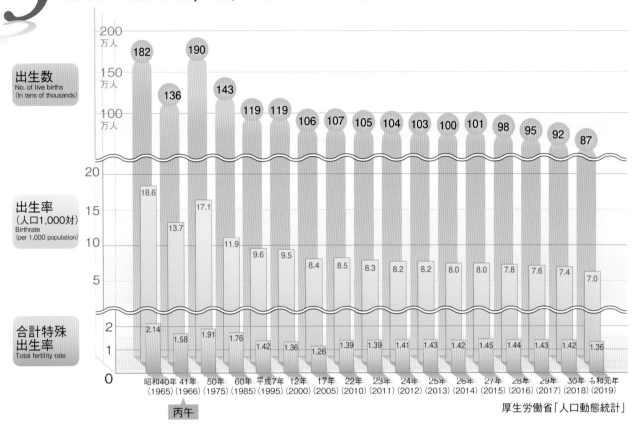

出生数
No. of live births
(In tens of thousands)

出生率
（人口1,000対）
Birthrate
(per 1,000 population)

合計特殊出生率
Total fertility rate

	昭和40年 (1965)	41年 (1966) 丙午	50年 (1975)	60年 (1985)	平成7年 (1995)	12年 (2000)	17年 (2005)	22年 (2010)	23年 (2011)	24年 (2012)	25年 (2013)	26年 (2014)	27年 (2015)	28年 (2016)	29年 (2017)	30年 (2018)	令和元年 (2019)
出生数	182	136	190	143	119	119	106	107	105	104	103	100	101	98	95	92	87
出生率	18.6	13.7	17.1	11.9	9.6	9.5	8.4	8.5	8.3	8.2	8.2	8.0	8.0	7.8	7.6	7.4	7.0
合計特殊出生率	2.14	1.58	1.91	1.76	1.42	1.36	1.26	1.39	1.39	1.41	1.43	1.42	1.45	1.44	1.43	1.42	1.36

厚生労働省「人口動態統計」

4 世帯員数の推移
Number of Household Members

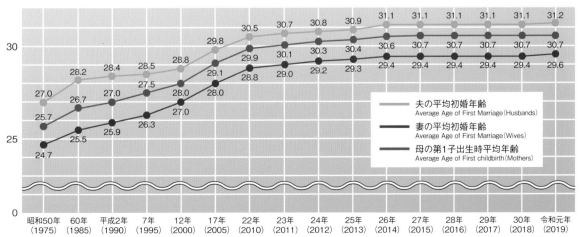

昭和35年 (1960)	45年 (1970)	55年 (1980)	平成2年 (1990)	12年 (2000)	17年 (2005)	22年 (2010)	23年 (2011)	24年 (2012)	25年 (2013)	26年 (2014)	27年 (2015)	28年 (2016)	29年 (2017)	30年 (2018)	令和元年 (2019)
4.13人	3.45人	3.28人	3.05人	2.76人	2.68人	2.59人	2.58人	2.57人	2.51人	2.49人	2.49人	2.47人	2.47人	2.44人	2.39人

※平成23年の数値は岩手県、宮城県及び福島県を、平成24年の数値は福島県を除いたもの　　厚生労働省「国民生活基礎調査」

5 初婚年齢の推移、初産年齢の推移
Change in Age of First Marriage and Age of First Childbirth

夫の平均初婚年齢
Average Age of First Marriage (Husbands)

妻の平均初婚年齢
Average Age of First Marriage (Wives)

母の第1子出生時平均年齢
Average Age of First childbirth (Mothers)

	昭和50年 (1975)	60年 (1985)	平成2年 (1990)	7年 (1995)	12年 (2000)	17年 (2005)	22年 (2010)	23年 (2011)	24年 (2012)	25年 (2013)	26年 (2014)	27年 (2015)	28年 (2016)	29年 (2017)	30年 (2018)	令和元年 (2019)
夫の平均初婚年齢	27.0	28.2	28.4	28.5	28.8	29.8	30.5	30.7	30.8	30.9	31.1	31.1	31.1	31.1	31.1	31.2
妻の平均初婚年齢	25.7	26.7	27.0	27.5	28.0	28.0	29.9	29.9	30.1	30.3	30.4	30.6	30.7	30.7	30.7	30.7
母の第1子出生時平均年齢	24.7	25.5	25.9	26.3	27.0	28.8	29.1	29.0	29.2	29.3	29.4	29.4	29.4	29.4	29.4	29.6

厚生労働省「人口動態統計」

（2）児童福祉行政 Child Welfare Administration

1 児童福祉行政のしくみ
Organizational Chart of the Child Welfare Administration

我が国の児童福祉行政は、国（所管：厚生労働省）、都道府県・指定都市を通じて行われます。具体的な業務の実行は、都道府県・指定都市等（注1）が設置する児童相談所を中心に、市区町村、保健所、福祉事務所などと役割を分担して行われています。児童相談所は広域を担うため、日常的な地域における子どもの福祉向上に関しては、市区町村の関連施策・施設や児童委員などが中心に担っています。

Japan's child welfare administration is conducted through the national level (jurisdiction: Ministry of Health, Labour and Welfare), prefectures and designated cities. Specific services are provided primarily at child guidance centers established in prefectures and designated cities, etc. (Note 1), with roles shared among municipalities, health centers, and welfare offices, etc. Since child guidance centers handle wide areas, matters concerning daily improvements in child welfare are handled primarily by related measures, facilities, and commissioned child welfare volunteers of the municipalities.

（注1）都道府県・指定都市の他に、全国2ヶ所の中核市が児童相談所を設置している。
(Note 1) In addition to prefectures and designated cities, child guidance centers have been established in two core cities throughout Japan.

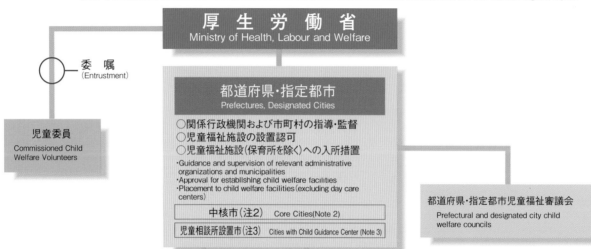

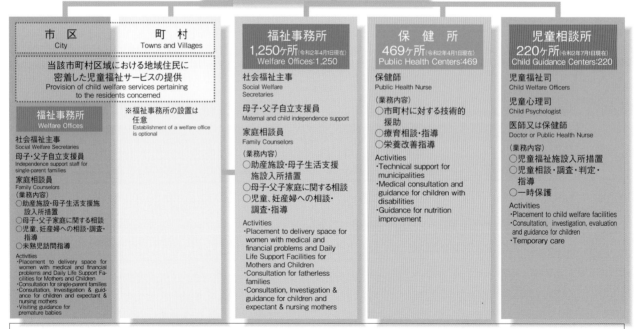

（注2）中核市　平成8年4月より、中核市が設けられ、特定児童福祉施設の設置認可等、一部の児童福祉行政について都道府県・指定都市の事務を行うこととされた。

(Note 2) Core cities were set up in April 1996 to handle a part of child welfare administration that is supposed to be conducted by prefectures and designated cities, such as approving establishment of specified child welfare facilities.

（注3）児童相談所設置市　平成18年4月より、児童相談所設置市（指定都市以外の市であって政令による指定を受けて児童相談所を設置する市）が設けられ、児童福祉施設への入所措置等、一部の児童福祉行政について、都道府県の事務を行うこととされた。なお、「児童福祉法等の一部を改正する法律」（平成28年法律第63号）において、平成29年4月より特別区についても政令の指定を受けて、児童相談所を設置することができることとされた。

(Note 3) Cities with child guidance center (cities specified by a Cabinet Order, other than designated cities, to establish a child guidance center) were set up in April 2006 to handle a part of child welfare administration that is supposed to be conducted by prefectures, such as placement of children to child welfare facilities. Under the revised Child Welfare Act (Act No. 63 of 2016), starting in April 2017, special wards are also allowed to establish a child guidance center if they are designated by a Cabinet Order.

2 主な児童福祉及び次世代育成関係法令
Main Laws Concerning Child Welfare and Raising the Next Generation

① 児童福祉法（昭和22年法律第164号）
② 少年法（昭和23年法律第168号）
③ 社会福祉法（昭和26年法律第45号）
④ 児童扶養手当法（昭和36年法律第238号）
⑤ 母子及び父子並びに寡婦福祉法（昭和39年法律第129号）
⑥ 特別児童扶養手当等の支給に関する法律（昭和39年法律第134号）
⑦ 母子保健法（昭和40年法律第141号）
⑧ 障害者基本法（昭和45年法律第84号）
⑨ 児童手当法（昭和46年法律第73号）
⑩ 児童買春、児童ポルノに係る行為等の規制及び処罰並びに児童の保護等に関する法律（平成11年法律第52号）
⑪ 児童虐待の防止等に関する法律（平成12年法律第82号）
⑫ 次世代育成支援対策推進法（平成15年法律第120号）
⑬ 少子化社会対策基本法（平成15年法律第133号）
⑭ 発達障害者支援法（平成16年法律第167号）
⑮ 障害者の日常生活及び社会生活を総合的に支援するための法律（平成17年法律第123号）
⑯ 子ども・子育て支援法（平成24年法律第65号）
⑰ 子どもの貧困対策の推進に関する法律（平成25年法律第64号）
⑱ 民間あっせん機関による養子縁組のあっせんに係る児童の保護等に関する法律（平成28年法律第110号）
⑲ 成育過程にある者及びその保護者並びに妊産婦に対し必要な成育医療等を切れ目なく提供するための施策の総合的な推進に関する法律（平成30年法律第104号）

① Child Welfare Act (Act No.164 of 1947)
② Juvenile Act (Act No. 168 of 1948)
③ Social Welfare Act (Act No. 45 of 1951)
④ Child Rearing Allowance Act (Act No. 238 of 1961)
⑤ Mother and Child, Father and Child and Widows Welfare Act (Act No.129 of 1964)
⑥ Act on Special Child Rearing Allowance(Act No.134 of 1964)
⑦ Maternal and Child Health Act (Act No.141 of 1965)
⑧ Basic Act for Persons with Disabilities (Act No. 84 of 1970)
⑨ Child Allowance Act (Act No.73 of 1971)
⑩ Act on Regulation and Punishment of Activities Relating to Child Prostitution and Child Pornography, and the Protection of Children (Act No.52 of 1999)
⑪ Act on the Prevention, etc. of Child Abuse (Act No.82 of 2000)
⑫ Act on Advancement of Measures to Support Raising Next-Generation Children (Act No.120 of 2003)
⑬ Basic Act for Measures to Cope with Society with Declining Birthrate (Act No. 133 of 2003)
⑭ Act on Support for Persons with Developmental Disabilities (Act No. 167 of 2004)
⑮ Comprehensive Support Act for Persons with Disabilities (Act No.123 of 2005)
⑯ Children and Childcare Support Act (Act No.65 of 2012)
⑰ Act on Promotion of Policy on Poverty among Children (Act No. 64 of 2013)
⑱ Act on Protection of Children Related to Adoptions Facilitated by the Private Adoption Agencies (Act No. 110 of 2016)
⑲ Basic Act for Child and Maternal Health and Child Development (Act No.104 of 2018)

3 児童福祉関係予算
Budget for Child Welfare Services

※18年度は三位一体改革により3,448億円を一般財源化
The sum of 344.8 billion yen was allotted for general finances in fiscal 2006 according to the three-in-one reform package.

※22年度は子ども手当創設により増加
In 2010 there was an increase due to the establishment of child allowance

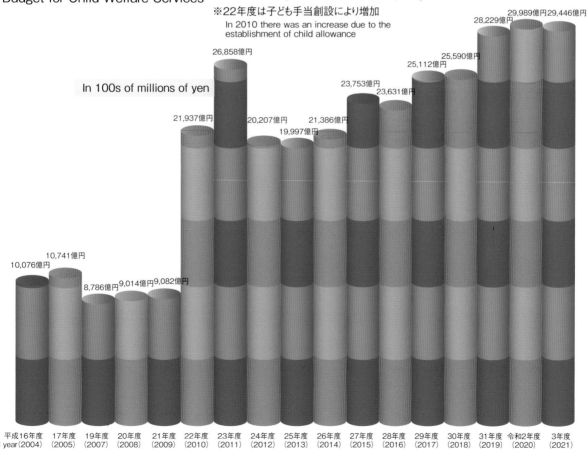

In 100s of millions of yen

平成16年度 Fiscal year(2004)	17年度(2005)	19年度(2007)	20年度(2008)	21年度(2009)	22年度(2010)	23年度(2011)	24年度(2012)	25年度(2013)	26年度(2014)	27年度(2015)	28年度(2016)	29年度(2017)	30年度(2018)	31年度(2019)	令和2年度(2020)	3年度(2021)
10,076億円	10,741億円	8,786億円	9,014億円	9,082億円	21,937億円	26,858億円	20,207億円	19,997億円	21,386億円	23,753億円	23,631億円	25,112億円	25,590億円	28,229億円	29,989億円	29,446億円

4 児童福祉施設
Child Welfare Facility

児童福祉施設の区分と機能

分　野	施設区分	機　能
A.母子保健の施策	1 助　産　施　設	保健上必要があるにもかかわらず、経済的理由により、入院助産を受けることができない妊産婦を入所させて、助産を受けさせる施設
B.保育の施策	2 保　育　所　等	保育を必要とする乳児・幼児を日々保護者の下から通わせて保育を行う施設
	(再掲)幼保連携型認定こども園	幼稚園と保育所の機能を併せ持ち、教育と保育を一体的に行う施設
C.子どもが健やかに育つための施策	3 児　童　館	屋内に集会室、遊戯室、図書室等必要な設備を設け、児童に健全な遊びを与えて、その健康を増進し、又は情操をゆたかにすることを目的とする施設
	4 児　童　遊　園	屋外に広場、ブランコ等必要な設備を設け、児童に健全な遊びを与えて、その健康を増進し、又は情操をゆたかにすることを目的とする施設
D.養護を必要とする子どもたちへの施策	5 乳　児　院	乳児を入院させて、これを養育し、あわせて退院した者について相談その他の援助を行う施設
	6 児童養護施設	保護者のない児童(乳児を除く)、虐待されている児童その他環境上養護を要する児童を入所させて、これを養護し、あわせて退所した者に対する相談その他の自立のための援助を行う施設
	7 児童心理治療施設	児童を短期間入所させ、又は保護者の下から通わせて、社会生活に適応するために必要な心理に関する治療、及び生活指導を主として行い、あわせて退所した者について相談その他の援助を行う施設
	8 児童自立支援施設	不良行為をなし、又はなすおそれのある児童及び家庭環境その他の環境上の理由により生活指導等を要する児童を入所させ、又は保護者の下から通わせて、個々の児童の状況に応じて必要な指導を行い、その自立を支援し、あわせて退所した者について相談その他の援助を行う施設
	9 児童家庭支援センター	地域の児童の福祉に関する各般の問題につき、児童に関する家庭その他からの相談に応じ、必要な助言、指導を行い、あわせて児童相談所、児童福祉施設等との連絡調整、援助を総合的に行う施設
	10 自立援助ホーム	義務教育を終了した20歳未満の児童等や大学在学中の者で、児童養護施設等を退所した者に対し、これらの者が共同生活を営む住居において、相談その他の日常生活上の援助、生活指導、就業の支援等を行う事業
	11 ファミリーホーム	養育者の家庭に児童を迎え入れて養育を行う家庭養護の一環として、保護者のない児童又は保護者に監護させることが不適当であると認められる児童に対し、養育を行う事業
E.ひとり親家庭への施策	12 母子生活支援施設	配偶者のない女子等及びその者の監護すべき児童を入所させて保護するとともに、自立の促進のため生活を支援し、あわせて退所した者について相談その他の援助を行う施設
F.障害児への施策	13 福祉型障害児入所施設	障害のある児童を入所させて、保護、日常生活の指導及び独立自活に必要な知識技能の付与を行う施設
	14 医療型障害児入所施設	障害のある児童を入所させて、保護、日常生活の指導、独立自活に必要な知識技能の付与及び治療を行う施設
	15 福祉型児童発達支援センター	障害のある児童を日々保護者の下から通わせて、日常生活における基本的動作の指導、独立自活に必要な知識技能の付与又は集団生活への適応のための訓練を行う施設
	16 医療型児童発達支援センター	障害のある児童を日々保護者の下から通わせて、日常生活における基本的動作の指導、独立自活に必要な知識技能の付与又は集団生活への適応のための訓練及び治療を行う施設

児童福祉関係施設と在所者数 令和元年10月1日 / 児童福祉施設の推移

施設区分	総数	公営	私営	在所者	昭和40年12月	昭和60年10月	平成17年10月	平成22年10月
1 助産施設	385 3,096	193 1,664	192 1,432	2,071 —	479 4,136	780 6,073	456 3,649	413 4,151
2 保育所等	28,737 2,792,277	8,296 849,757	20,441 1,942,520	2,586,393 —	11,199 876,140	22,899 2,078,765	22,624 2,060,938	21,681 2,033,292
(再掲)幼保連携型認定こども園	5,144 518,219	736 74,521	4,408 443,698	511,590 —	— —	— —	— —	— —
3 児童館	4,453 —	2,553 —	1,900 —	— 	544 	3,517 	4,716 	4,345
4 児童遊園	2,221 	2,166 	55 	— 	— 	4,173 	3,802 	3,283
5 乳児院	142 3,868	5 109	137 3,759	2,931 —	127 3,859	122 4,064	117 3,669	125 3,778
6 児童養護施設	609 31,311	9 377	600 30,934	25,534 —	578 38,667	572 37,088	558 33,676	582 34,215
7 児童心理治療施設	49 2,109	5 200	44 1,909	1,422 —	4 200	11 550	27 1,323	37 1,709
8 児童自立支援施設	58 3,561	56 3,426	2 135	1,236 —	58 6,276	57 4,989	58 4,227	58 4,029
9 児童家庭支援センター	130 —	— —	130 —	— —	— 	— 	57 	75
10 自立援助ホーム	176 1,148	— —	176 1,148	573 —	— 	— 	— 	73 491
11 ファミリーホーム	417 2,481	— —	417 2,481	1,574 —	— 	— 	— 	104 613
12 母子生活支援施設	219 4,547	28 492	191 4,055	8,095 —	621 12,768	348 6,938	282 5,648	262 5,409
13 福祉型障害児入所施設	255 9,477	37 1,514	218 7,963	6,925 —	— —	— —	— —	— —
14 医療型障害児入所施設	218 20,622	78 7,112	140 1,351	9,378 —	— —	— —	— —	— —
15 福祉型児童発達支援センター	601 18,659	132 5,197	469 13,462	35,052 —	— —	— —	— —	— —
16 医療型児童発達支援センター	98 3,197	48 1,597	50 1,600	2,061 —	— —	— —	— —	— —
総数	38,701 2,895,944	13,606 871,445	25,095 2,012,340	2,681,174 —	13,610 942,046	32,479 2,138,467	32,697 2,113,130	31,038 2,087,687

※児童養護施設の推移については、児童養護施設の値に虚弱児施設の値を加えたものである。幼保連携型認定こども園については保育所部分のみである。また、⑬〜⑯の推移については、平成24年度に施行された改正児童福祉法により施設体系が整理されたことから、未記入となっている。
厚生労働省「社会福祉施設等調査」 ※⑩は厚生労働省家庭福祉課調べ(平成30年10月1日)、⑪は「福祉行政報告例」(令和元年度)

4 Child Welfare Facility

Categories and Functions of Child Welfare Facilities

Area	Category	Functions
A.Maternal and Child Health	1 Delivery Spaces (for women with medical and financial problems)	To provide medical care for pregnant women in need of both medical and financial support
B.Day Care	2 Day-care Centers	Facilities where parents/guardians take their infant/child to receive childcare services on a daily basis
	(regrouped) Centers for Early Childhood Education and Care (integrated center model)	Facilities that provide integrated education and childcare services with functions of both a kindergarten and a day care center
C.Measures for Enabling Children to Grow up Healthy	3 Children's Halls	Facilities consisting of important features, such as indoor meeting rooms, play rooms, and libraries, for the purpose of promoting children's health by providing them with an opportunity to play in a way that benefits health and enriching their emotional development.
	4 Children's Playground	Facilities consisting of important features, such as outdoor spaces and swings, for the purpose of promoting children's health by providing them with an opportunity to play in a way that benefits health and enriching their emotional development.
D.Measures for Children who Require Protective Care,etc	5 Homes for infants	To care for babies without guardians
	6 Children's Homes	Facilities that admit and provide protective care for children (excluding infants) without a guardian, children who have been abused, and other children in need of protective care in terms of their environment, as well as providing consultation and other independence support for those who have left there.
	7 Psychological Treatment Facilities for Children	Facilities that admit children for a short term or have them commute from their guardians. They mainly provide psychological treatment and guidance in daily living so that the children can adapt themselves to social life. They also provide consultation and other assistance for those who have left there.
	8 Support Facilities for Development of Self-sustaining Capacity	To support children's independence and provide guidance to children committing or liable to commit delinquent acts, or children need advices for life due to their family environment and other reasons
	9 Children and families supporting center	To provide comprehensive support, including: counseling and guidance on child welfare in a community and coordination with other relevant organizations
	10 Homes supporting independence	Facilities that provide consultation, other support and guidance in daily living, as well as employment assistance in the communal environment for those who have left children's homes. The residents include those aged below 20 who have completed compulsory education and those in college.
	11 Family homes	To provide care by guardians in a family setting to children whose parents are unavailable or considered unsuitable to take care of them
E.Measures for Single-Parent Families	12 Daily Life Support Facilities for Mothers and Children	To provide institutional care to protect mothers and children of fatherless families and to promote their independence as well as to provide support to those who left the facility
F.Services for Disabled Children	13 Facilities for Disabled Child Placement	Facilities where disabled children are placed which provide them with care, guidance for daily life, and the knowledge and skills necessary to live independent lives
	14 Facilities for Disabled Child Placement with Medical Services	Facilities where disabled children are placed which, in addition to medical treatment, provide them with care, guidance for daily life, and the knowledge and skills necessary to live independent lives
	15 Child Development Support Centers	Facilities that disabled children who live at home visit daily which provide them with guidance with basic activities for daily living, the knowledge and skills necessary to live independent lives, and training for adapting to group living
	16 Child Development Support Centers with Medical Services	Facilities that disabled children who live at home visit daily which, in addition to medical treatment, provide them with guidance with basic activities for daily living, the knowledge and skills necessary to live independent lives, and training for adapting to group living

No. of child welfare facilities and no. of capacity and children actually registered October 1, 2019

Changes in no. of child welfare facilities

	Category	Total	Public	Private	No.of children registered	(1965)	(1985)	(2005)	(2010)
1	Delivery Spaces (for women with medical and financial problems)	385 3,096	193 1,664	192 1,432	2,071 ―	479 4,136	780 6,073	456 3,649	413 4,151
2	Day-care Centers	28,737 2,792,277	8,296 849,757	20,441 1,942,520	2,586,393 ―	11,199 876,140	22,899 2,078,765	22,624 2,060,938	21,681 2,033,292
	(regrouped) Centers for Early Childhood Education and Care by collaboration of kindergarten and day care center models	5,144 518,219	736 74,521	4,408 443,698	511,590 ―	― ―	― ―	― ―	― ―
3	Children's Halls	4,453 ―	2,553 ―	1,900 ―		544 ―	3,517 ―	4,716 ―	4,345 ―
4	Children's Playground	2,221 ―	2,166 ―	55 ―		― ―	4,173 ―	3,802 ―	3,283 ―
5	Homes for infants	142 3,868	5 109	137 3,759	2,931 ―	127 3,859	122 4,064	117 3,669	125 3,778
6	Children's Homes	609 31,311	9 377	600 30,934	25,534 ―	578 38,667	572 37,088	558 33,676	582 34,215
7	Psychological treatment facilities for children	49 2,109	5 200	44 1,909	1,422 ―	4 200	11 550	27 1,323	37 1,709
8	Support Facilities for Development of Self-sustaining Capacity	58 3,561	56 3,426	2 135	1,236 ―	58 6,276	57 4,989	58 4,227	58 4,029
9	Children and families supporting center	130 ―	― ―	130 ―		― ―	― ―	57 ―	75 ―
10	Homes supporting independence	176 1,148	― ―	176 1,148	573 ―	― ―	― ―	― ―	73 491
11	Family homes	417 2,481	― ―	417 2,481	1,574 ―	― ―	― ―	― ―	104 613
12	Daily Life Support Facilities for Mothers and Children	219 4,547	28 492	191 4,055	8,095 ―	621 12,768	348 6,938	282 5,648	262 5,409
13	Facilities for Disabled Child Placement	255 9,477	37 1,514	218 7,963	6,925 ―	― ―	― ―	― ―	― ―
14	Facilities for Disabled Child Placement with Medical Services	218 20,622	78 7,112	140 1,351	9,378 ―	― ―	― ―	― ―	― ―
15	Child Development Support Centers	601 18,659	132 5,197	469 13,462	35,052 ―	― ―	― ―	― ―	― ―
16	Child Development Support Centers with Medical Services	98 3,197	48 1,597	50 1,600	2,061 ―	― ―	― ―	― ―	― ―
	Total	38,701 2,895,944	13,606 871,445	25,095 2,012,340	2,681,174 ―	13,610 942,046	32,479 2,138,467	32,697 2,113,130	31,038 2,087,687

※The past data of numbers of Children's Home include numbers of Home for Physically Weak Children. Data on Centers for Early Childhood Education and Care (integrated center model) include those of the day care center model only.
　No data is listed under changes in the number of child welfare facilities for categories 13 to 16 because these facilities were organized under the revised Child Welfare Act which went into effect in 2012.

5 児童相談所の機能と活動状況
Functions and Activities of Child Guidance Center

児童相談所と関係機関図
Child Guidance Center and related agencies

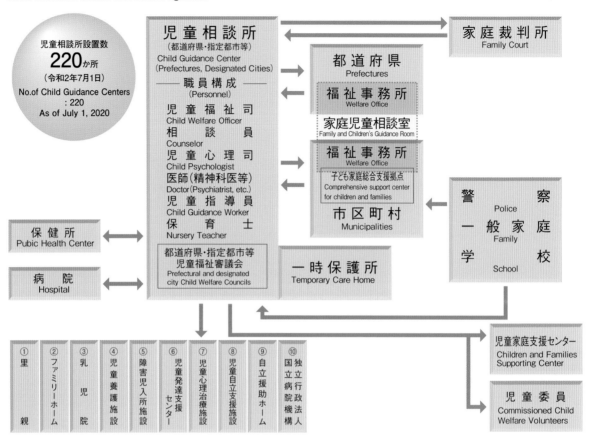

①Foster Parent ②Family Home ③Home for Infant ④Children's Home ⑤Disabled child placement facilities ⑥Child development support centers ⑦Psychological treatment facilities for children ⑧Support Facility for Development of Self-sustaining Capacity ⑨Home for Supporting Independent Living ⑩National Hospital Organization

6 児童相談所における相談対応件数の推移
The Number of Consultations at Child Guidance Centers

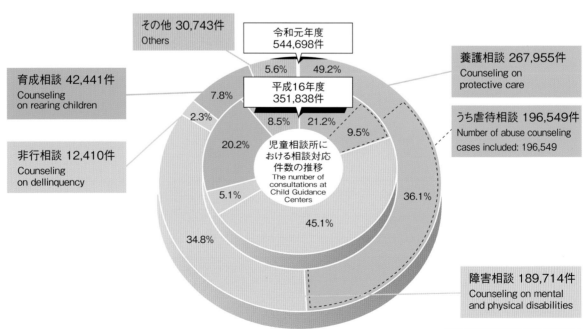

その他 30,743件
Others

育成相談 42,441件
Counseling on rearing children

非行相談 12,410件
Counseling on dellinquency

令和元年度 544,698件

平成16年度 351,838件

養護相談 267,955件
Counseling on protective care

うち虐待相談 196,549件
Number of abuse counseling cases included: 196,549

障害相談 189,714件
Counseling on mental and physical disabilities

児童相談所における相談対応件数の推移
The number of consultations at Child Guidance Centers

5.6%　49.2%
7.8%
2.3%　8.5%　21.2%
9.5%
20.2%
36.1%
5.1%
45.1%
34.8%

厚生労働省「福祉行政報告例」

（3）子ども・子育て支援と仕事と家庭の両立　Child and Child-rearing Support and Establishing Compatibility between Work and Family Life

「少子化社会対策大綱」は、少子化社会対策基本法に基づく「大綱」（基本的な内容）として、令和2年5月29日に閣議決定されました。「少子化社会対策大綱」に基づき、社会全体で子育てを支え、結婚や出産、子育ての希望が叶えられるよう、各種施策を推進しています。また、地方自治体や事業主においては、次世代育成支援のための行動計画を策定し、集中的・計画的な取り組みを推進しています。

"Outline of Measures to Cope with Society with Decreasing Birthrate" is a May 29, 2020 cabinet decision, with the "general framework" (basic details) based on the Basic Act for Measures to Cope with Society with declining Birthrate. Based on "Outline of Measures to Cope with Society with Decreasing Birthrate", this initiative provides society-wide support for child-rearing, and promotes measures to help citizens realize their hopes of marriage, childbirth, and child-rearing. The initiative also promotes formulation of action plans and concentrative and planned efforts for local governments and business owners to support the development of the next generation.

1 次世代育成支援対策推進法（平成17年度から令和6年度までの時限立法）
Act on Advancement of Measures to Support Raising Next-Generation Children （Temporary Statute from FY 2005 to FY 2024）

行動計画策定指針
Action Plan Formulation Guideline

●国において地方公共団体及び事業主が行動計画を策定する際の指針を策定
・National guidelines are to be set for regional public organizations and business owners to follow when formulating action plans.

地方公共団体行動計画の策定
Local Public Organization Action Plans

①市町村行動計画
②都道府県行動計画
1. Municipal Action Plans
2. Prefectural Action Plans

地域住民の意見の反映、労使の参画、計画の内容・実施状況の公表、定期的な評価・見直し 等
Reflection of opinions of local residents, labour-management participation, publication of plan details and implementation status, regular evaluation/review, etc.

平成27年度から子ども・子育て支援法に基づく事業計画等の策定が義務化されたことに伴い、次世代育成支援対策推進法に基づく地方公共団体行動計画の策定が任意化された
Development of local public organization action plans under Act on Advancement of Measures to Support Raising Next-Generation Children became optional as development of plans became mandatory in FY 2015 based on the Act on Support for Children and Child-rearing.

事業主等行動計画の策定・公表・周知
Formulation, Publication and Dissemination of Action Plans by Business Owners and Others

①一般事業主行動計画（企業等がその社員等にむけて）
●大企業（301人以上）：義務
●中小企業（101人以上）：義務（23年4月〜）
●中小企業（100人以下）：努力義務
●一定の基準を満たした企業を認定
②特定事業主行動計画（国・地方公共団体がその職員等にむけて）

1. General business owner action plan (for companies to present to their employees)
・Big-sized corporations with more than 301 employees: compulsory
・Medium-and small-sized corporations with 101or more employees: compulsory (April 2011)
・Medium-and small-sized corporations with less than 100 employees: Efforts compulsory
・Companies that fulfill the set standards will be certified
2. Specific business owner action plan (for national and local public institutions to present to their staff)

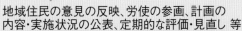

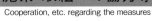

施策・取組への協力等
Cooperation, etc. regarding the measures

策定支援等
Formulation of support, etc.

次世代育成支援対策地域協議会
Regional Next Generation Nurturing Support Measures Conferences

●都道府県、市町村、事業主、労働者、社会福祉・教育関係者等が組織
Organized by prefectures, cities, business owners, workers, social welfare and education related affiliates,and others

次世代育成支援対策推進センター
Next Generation Nurturing Support Measures Promotion Center

●経済団体による情報提供、相談等の実施
Provision of related information and consultation services by economic organizations

2 少子化社会対策大綱（令和2年5月29日閣議決定）
～新しい令和の時代にふさわしい少子化対策へ～

Outline of Measures to Cope with Society with Decreasing Birthrate (approved in a Cabinet meeting on May 29, 2020)
- Measures against the Declining Birthrate Appropriate to the New Reiwa Era -

背景　Background

○少子化の進行は、人口（特に生産年齢人口）の減少と高齢化を通じて、社会経済に多大な影響
○少子化の主な原因は、未婚化・晩婚化、有配偶出生率の低下
○背景には、個々人の結婚や出産、子育ての希望の実現を阻む様々な要因
○希望の実現を阻む隘路を打破するため、長期的な展望に立ち、必要な安定財源を確保しながら、総合的な少子化対策を大胆に進める必要
○新型コロナウイルス感染症の流行は、安心して子供を生み育てられる環境整備の重要性を改めて浮き彫りにした　学校の臨時休業等により影響を受ける子育て世帯に対する支援等の対策と併せて、非常時の対応にも留意しながら総合的な少子化対策を進める

○A declining birthrate has significant socioeconomic effects through population decline (especially working- age population) and aging.
○Major causes of the declining birthrate include more people never marrying or marrying late, as well as a declining birthrate among married couples.
○Various barriers prevent individuals from realizing their wishes regarding marriage, childbirth, and child-rearing.
○In order to remove these barriers, comprehensive and bold measures against the declining birthrate are needed, from a long-term perspective and with stable funding.
○The COVID-19 pandemic has reminded people of the importance of safe and reassuring environments for childbirth and child-rearing.
Along with support for families with children affected by the temporary school closure, comprehensive measures against the declining birthrate will be promoted while taking account of emergency response.

基本的な目標　Fundamental Goals

○「希望出生率1.8」の実現に向け、令和の時代にふさわしい環境を整備し、国民が結婚、妊娠・出産、子育てに希望を見出せるとともに、男女が互いの生き方を尊重しつつ、主体的な選択により、希望する時期に結婚でき、かつ、希望するタイミングで希望する数の子供を持てる社会をつくる（結婚、妊娠・出産、子育ては個人の自由な意思決定に基づくものであり、個々人の決定に特定の価値観を押し付けたり、プレッシャーを与えたりすることがあってはならないことに十分留意）

○To develop an environment appropriate to the Reiwa era with the aim of achieving a desired birthrate of 1.8, thereby building a society that enables people to find hope in marriage, pregnancy, childbirth, and child-rearing; to make their own decision on when to marry while respecting their partner's lifestyle, and to have choices on family planning. (giving full consideration to the facts that marriage, pregnancy, childbirth, and child-rearing should be based on individuals' free will and that no specific value should be pressed on them)

基本的な考え方　Basic Concept

1 結婚・子育て世代が将来にわたる展望を描ける環境をつくる
○若い世代が将来に展望を持てる雇用環境等の整備
○結婚を希望する者への支援
○男女共に仕事と子育てを両立できる環境の整備
○子育て等により離職した女性の再就職支援、地域活動への参画支援
○男性の家事・育児参画の促進
○働き方改革と暮らし方改革

1 Develop an environment that enables people to have bright prospects for the future on marriage and parenthood
○Developing an employment environment that enables young people to have bright prospects for the future
○Supporting people who want to marry
○Developing an environment that enables both men and women to balance work and child-rearing
○Helping women, who left their jobs to care for children, to return to work and participate in community activities
○Encouraging men to participate in housework and childcare
○Reforming work styles and lifestyles

2 多様化する子育て家庭の様々なニーズに応える
○子育てに関する支援（経済的支援、心理的・肉体的負担の軽減等）
○在宅子育て家庭に対する支援
○多子世帯、多胎児を育てる家庭に対する支援
○妊娠期から子育て期にわたる切れ目のない支援
○子育ての担い手の多様化と世代間での助け合い

2 Address various needs of increasingly diverse child-rearing families
○Supporting child-rearing (economic support, reducing emotional and physical burdens, etc.)
○Supporting families raising children at home
○Supporting families with 3 or more children
○Providing seamless support from pregnancy to child-rearing
○Involving more people in child-rearing and promoting inter-generational mutual support

3 地域の実情に応じたきめ細かな取組を進める
○結婚、子育てに関する地方公共団体の取組に対する支援
○地方創生と連携した取組の推進

3 Promote initiatives tailored to each community
○Supporting municipalities' initiatives on marriage and child-rearing
○Promoting initiatives collaborating with regional revitalization programs

4 結婚、妊娠・出産、子供・子育てに温かい社会をつくる
○結婚を希望する人を応援し、子育て世帯をやさしく包み込む社会的機運の醸成
○妊娠中の方や子供連れに優しい施設や外出しやすい環境の整備
○結婚、妊娠・出産、子供・子育てに関する効果的な情報発信

4 Build a supportive society for marriage, pregnancy, childbirth, children, and child-rearing
○Creating an atmosphere conducive to people who want to marry and child-rearing families
○Developing facilities and environments friendly to pregnant women and families with small children
○Disseminating useful information on marriage, pregnancy, childbirth, children, and child-rearing

5 科学技術の成果など新たなリソースを積極的に活用する
○結婚支援・子育て分野におけるICTやAI等の科学技術の成果の活用促進

5 Actively use new resources, including advanced technologies
○Promoting the use of advanced technologies such as ICT and AI in marriage support and child-rearing

このほか、ライフステージ（結婚前、結婚、妊娠・出産、子育て）ごとに施策の方向性を整理
Setting the direction of other measures for each life stage (e.g., before marriage, marriage, pregnancy, childbirth, and child-rearing)

施策の推進体制等　Systems to Promote Measures

○有識者の意見を聞きつつ、施策の進捗状況等を検証・評価する体制を構築し、PDCAサイクルを適切に回す
○施策について数値目標を設定するとともに、その進捗を定期的にフォローアップ
○更に強力に少子化対策を推し進めるために必要な安定財源の確保について、国民各層の理解を得ながら、社会全体での費用負担の在り方を含め、幅広く検討

○A system will be developed to examine and evaluate the progress of the measures, while obtaining experts' input, and will be managed through the effective use of the PDCA cycle.
○Numerical targets will be set for the measures, with regular follow-ups on their progress.
○Extensive discussion will be conducted on methods of securing stable funding essential for further measures against the declining birthrate, including how to bear expenses as the entire society, while obtaining wide support from people.

結婚支援　Marriage support

○地方公共団体による総合的な結婚支援の取組に対する支援

〔自治体間連携を伴う広域的な結婚支援に対する重点的支援〕

- AIを始めとするマッチングシステムの高度化や相談員による支援を組み合わせた結婚支援の取組等に対し、補助率を嵩上げ（1/2→2/3）

〔結婚新生活支援事業の充実〕

- 年齢・年収要件の緩和（34歳以下→39歳以下、世帯年収480万円相当→540万円相当）
- 都道府県が主導して管内市区町村における本事業の面的拡大を図る優れた取組については、上記の緩和に加え、補助上限額を引き上げる（30万円→29歳以下60万円）とともに、補助率を嵩上げ（1/2→2/3）

○Assistance for local authorities' comprehensive initiatives on marriage support
〔Intensive assistance for inter-municipality initiatives on marriage support〕
- Increasing the subsidy rate (1/2 → 2/3) for marriage support initiatives that combine multiple methods (e.g., an enhanced matching system using AI and in-person support by counselors)
〔Enhancement of livelihood support for newlyweds〕
- Easing eligibility criteria (age: 34 or below → 39 or below; annual household income: 4.8M yen → 5.4M yen)
- Increasing the maximum subsidy (0.3M yen → 0.6M yen for those aged 29 or below) and the subsidy rate (1/2 → 2/3), besides the above revision, for excellent initiatives led by prefectures to comprehensively expand municipal support programs

妊娠・出産への支援　Pregnancy and childbirth support

○不妊治療等への支援

〔不妊治療への経済的支援〕

- 現行の助成制度の拡充

〔不妊治療を受けやすい職場環境整備〕

- 社会的機運の醸成（企業・職場や社会の理解促進）
- 不妊治療と仕事の両立のための職場環境の整備(事業主の取組促進)
- 中小企業向け助成金による中小企業の取組支援
- 企業が策定する行動計画の指針の改正を関係審議会で検討中　等

〔不妊症・不育症への相談支援等〕

- 不妊専門相談センターにおける相談支援体制の強化　等

〔不育症への経済的支援〕

- 不育症検査への助成金の創設

○妊娠期から子育て期にわたる切れ目のない支援

〔子育て世代包括支援センターの強化〕

- 困難事例への対応等支援に要する人員の追加配置

〔産後ケア事業の全国展開〕

○Support for infertility treatment, etc.
〔Economic support for infertility treatment〕
- Enhancing the existing subsidy system
〔Development of supportive workplace environments for infertility treatment〕
- Creating a conducive atmosphere (promoting awareness in companies, workplaces, and society)
- Developing workplace environments that enable people to balance infertility treatment and work (promoting initiatives by employers)
- Supporting smaller businesses' initiatives through subsidies
- Discussions being in progress at relevant councils on revision of guidelines for companies' action plans
〔Counseling and support on infertility〕
- Enhancing counseling and support systems at infertility counseling centers
〔Economic support for infertility〕
- Establishing a subsidy system for infertility tests
○Seamless support from pregnancy to child-rearing
〔Enhancement of comprehensive support centers for families with children〕
- Adding staff to handle difficult cases
〔Nationwide expansion of postnatal care programs〕

仕事と子育ての両立支援　Support for balancing work and child-rearing

○待機児童の解消

「新子育て安心プラン」の実施

- 令和3〜6年度の4年間で約14万人分の保育の受け皿を整備
- 企業主導型ベビーシッターの利用補助の拡充（1日2,200円→4,400円）
- 育児休業等取得に積極的に取り組む中小企業に対する50万円の助成事業を創設　等

○男性の育児休業の取得促進

- 出生直後の休業の取得を促進する新たな枠組みの導入、妊娠・出産の申出をした個別の労働者に対する休業制度の周知の措置等を関係審議会で検討中

○Reduction of the number of children on nursery waiting lists
Implementation of the New National Plan on Child-Rearing
- Increasing nursery capacity by approx. 140,000 over 4 years (FY2021-2024)
- Increasing the subsidy for users of company-led babysitting services (2,200 yen/day → 4,400 yen)
- Establishing a subsidy program for smaller businesses actively promoting the use of childcare leave (0.5M yen)
○Initiatives to encourage men to take childcare leave
- Discussions being in progress at relevant councils on measures, including the introduction of new frameworks to promote men's use of postnatal leave and information dissemination on leave systems to individual workers who notify pregnancy and childbirth

地域・社会による子育て支援　Child-rearing support by communities and society

○多機能型地域子育て支援の新たな展開

〔利用者支援事業〕

- 地域の支援員が各事業所等を巡回し、連携・協働の体制づくり等の支援を実施

〔ファミリー・サポート・センター事業〕

- 安心して子どもの預かり等を実施するため、地域子育て支援拠点等との連携を強化

〔地域子育て支援拠点事業〕

- 両親共に参加しやすくなるよう、休日の育児参加促進に関する講習会実施を支援　等

○New development of multifunctional community-based child-rearing support
〔User support programs〕
- Local support staff visiting providers and helping them build collaborative systems
〔Family support centers〕
- Enhancing collaboration with community-based child-rearing support centers and others to ensure childcare support
〔Community-based child-rearing support centers〕
- Helping the centers organize workshops to encourage both parents to participate in childcare on days off

経済的支援　Economic support

○税制

- 結婚・子育て資金の一括贈与に係る贈与税の非課税措置の延長等

【適用期限：令和5年3月末まで】

- 国や地方自治体の実施する子育てに係る助成等（*）の非課税措置

*地方自治体等が行う子育て支援に係るベビーシッターの利用料等の助成

- 産後ケア事業に要する費用に係る税制措置の創設（消費税、地方消費税）

○Tax
- Extending the tax exemption period regarding lump sum gifts for marriage and child-rearing [until March 31, 2023]
- Providing tax exemptions for child-rearing subsidies from national and local governments
*Providing subsidies for users of babysitting services organized by municipalities and others as part of the child-rearing support
- Establishing a tax system on costs needed for postnatal care programs (consumption tax, local consumption tax)

新型コロナウイルス感染症への対応　Responses to the COVID-19 pandemic

- 不安を抱え困難な状況にある妊産婦への相談支援等の実施
- 保育所等及び地域子ども・子育て支援事業における感染拡大防止対策に係る支援

- Providing counseling and support for pregnant women and nursing mothers in difficulties with anxiety
- Supporting infection control measures in nurseries as well as local child and child-rearing support programs

※検討事項とされた項目を含め、大綱に基づく施策の進捗状況等について、PDCAサイクルを通じたフォローアップを実施。
※The progress of these measures based on the Outline, including those under discussion, will be followed up through the PDCA cycle.

3 子ども・子育て支援新制度

The comprehensive support system for children and child-rearing

平成24年3月に少子化社会対策会議において決定した「子ども・子育て新システムに関する基本制度」等に基づき、同年の通常国会において子ども・子育て支援法をはじめとする「子ども・子育て関連3法」が成立しました。これらの法律に基づき、平成27年度より「子ども・子育て支援新制度」が実施されています。

子ども・子育て支援新制度は、家族構成の変化や地域のつながりの希薄化による子育て家庭の不安や孤立感、深刻な待機児童問題、急激な少子化の進行等の子どもや子育てをめぐる厳しい環境のなか、安心して子どもを産み、育てることのできる社会の実現という社会全体で取り組まなければならない最重要課題の一つに対応するために実施されています。

Based on "The Basic System for the New System for Children and Child-rearing" decided upon at the Conference on Measures for Society with a Declining Birthrate in March 2012, "Three laws on children and child-rearing" such as child and Childcare Support Act were approved at the ordinary Diet in the same year. The Comprehensive Support System for Children and Child-rearing started in FY 2015 based on these laws.

The recent social environment is not supportive to have and raise children: Many families feel insecure and lonely due to drastic changes in family structure and weakening community ties, there is a serious problem with long waiting lists for day care, and the birth rate is declining sharply. In this difficult environment, the new system has been implemented to respond to one of the most important challenges for the entire society: to build a society where parents can have and nurture children without worry.

【基本的な考え方】【Basic Philosophy】

■ 子ども・子育て関連3法の趣旨
　○幼児期の学校教育・保育、地域の子ども・子育て支援を総合的に推進
■ 基本的な方向性
　○認定こども園、幼稚園、保育所を通じた共通の給付（「施設型給付」）及び小規模保育等への給付（「地域型保育給付」）の創設
　○認定こども園制度の改善（幼保連携型認定こども園の改善等）
　　・幼保連携型認定こども園について、認可・指導監督の一本化、学校及び児童福祉施設としての法的位置づけ
　○地域の子ども・子育て支援の充実（利用者支援、地域子育て支援拠点など）
■ 幼児期の学校教育・保育、地域の子ども・子育て支援に共通の仕組み
　○基礎自治体（市町村）が実施主体
　　・市町村は地域のニーズに基づき計画を策定、給付・事業を実施
　　・国・都道府県は実施主体の市町村を重層的に支える
　○社会全体による費用負担
　　・消費税率の引き上げによる、国及び地方の恒久財源の確保を前提
　　（幼児教育・保育・子育て支援の質・量の拡充を図るためには、消費税率の引き上げにより確保する0.7兆円程度を含めて1兆円超程度の財源が必要）
　○政府の推進体制
　　・制度ごとにバラバラな政府の推進体制を整備（子ども・子育て本部の設置など内閣府を中心とした一元的体制を整備）
　○子ども・子育て会議の設置
　　・有識者、地方公共団体、事業主代表・労働者代表、子育て当事者、子育て支援当事者等が、子育て支援の政策プロセス等に参画・関与
　　・市町村等の合議制機関（地方版子ども・子育て会議）の設置努力義務

■ Purposes of the Three Acts Enacted
　○To comprehensively promote the support of education and care during early childhood as well as support local children and child-rearing.
■ Basic Direction of the Acts
　○Establish a common allowance for centers for early childhood education and care, kindergartens, and day care centers (institutional allowance), as well as a small-sized day care allowance (local childcare allowance).
　○Improvement of the system on centers for early childhood education and care (improvement of the integrated center model, etc.)
　　・Integrate licensing, guidance and supervision of centers for early childhood education and care (integrated center model), and providing them with the legal status as schools and child welfare facilities.
　○To enhance support of children and child-rearing (local child-rearing support programs, local child-rearing support bases, etc.)
■ Common framework for the support of education and care during early childhood as well as support local children and child-rearing
　○Local municipalities function as the main constituents that provide support
　　・Local municipalities will develop plans based on regional needs to provide allowances and implement support programs.
　　・The national government and prefectural governments will provide support to municipalities at multiple levels.
　○Society-wide cost burden
　　・Support premised on securing a permanent source of funds at both the national and regional level by increasing the consumption tax rate.
　　(In order to increase the quality and amount of support for childhood education, day care, and child-rearing, 1 trillion yen is necessary which includes 700 billion yen secured by increasing the consumption tax rate.)
　○Government Implementation System
　　・Create an integrated government implementation system (creation of an integrated system centering on the Cabinet Office (establishment of a child and child-rearing government office, etc.))
　○Establishment of the Child and Child-rearing Conference
　　・Experts, local governments, business representatives, labor representatives, persons concerned with raising children, persons concerned with child-rearing support and other parties participate in the policy-making process, etc. regarding child-rearing support.
　　・Municipalities (Local Governments) have the obligation to make efforts to establish council organizations (the Local Child and Child-rearing Conference).

【給付・事業の全体像】【Overall Picture of Allowances and Services】

子ども・子育て支援給付
Allowances for Child-Rearing Support Services

■ 施設型給付
　・認定こども園、幼稚園、保育所を通じた共通の給付
　※私立保育所については、現行どおり、市町村が保育所に委託費を支払い、利用者負担の徴収も市町村が行うものとする
■ 地域型保育給付
　・家庭的保育、小規模保育、居宅訪問型保育、事業所内保育
　※施設型給付・地域型保育給付は、夜間・休日保育にも対応
■ 施設等利用給付
　・幼稚園〈未移行〉、認可外保育施設、預かり保育等の利用に係る支援
■ 児童手当

■ Institutional allowance
　・Common allowance for centers for early childhood education and care, kindergartens, and day care centers.
　Note: As for private day care centers, municipalities will continue to pay consignment fees and shall also conduct related fee collections.
■ Local childcare allowance
　・Home-based day care, small-sized day care, home-visit day care, and workplace day care
　Note: The institutional allowance and the local childcare allowance will cover evening and weekend childcare.
■ Facility use allowance
　・Support related to use of kindergartens (under the old system), non-licensed day care facilities, temporary childcare, etc.
■ Child allowance

地域子ども・子育て支援事業
Local Child and Child-rearing Support Programs

①利用者支援事業、②延長保育事業、③実費徴収に係る補足給付を行う事業、④多様な事業者の参入促進・能力活用事業、⑤放課後児童健全育成事業（放課後児童クラブ）、⑥子育て短期支援事業、⑦乳児家庭全戸訪問事業、⑧養育支援訪問事業・子どもを守る地域ネットワーク機能強化事業、⑨地域子育て支援拠点事業、⑩一時預かり事業、⑪病児保育事業、⑫子育て援助活動支援事業（ファミリー・サポート・センター事業）、⑬妊婦健康診査

①Support for clients, ②extended day care, ③supplemental benefits to cover expenses, ④programs to encourage various providers to enter this field and to utilize their capacity, ⑤after-school child sound upbringing services (after-school children's clubs), ⑥ short-term child care support services, ⑦visit to all families with a baby, ⑧enhancement of home-visiting childcare support and of local networks to protect children, ⑨community-based childrearing support center, ⑩temporary custody, ⑪childcare for children with disease, ⑫support for childcare assistance (Family Support Centers), ⑬health checkups for pregnant women

※出産・育児に係る休業に伴う給付（仮称）→将来の検討課題　　Note: Allowances accompanying leaves of absence for childbirth and nursing (provisional name) is subject to future examination.

【新制度による教育・保育の提供のしくみ】
【Framework for providing education and day care through the new system】

共通の財政支援 Common Financial Support

「施設型給付」（認定こども園、幼稚園、保育所）等と「地域型保育給付」（小規模保育事業、家庭的保育事業、居宅訪問型事業、事業所内保育事業）を創設する。

Establishment of the institutional allowance (includes centers for early childhood education and care, kindergartens, and day care centers) and the local childcare allowance (small-sized day care, home-based day care, home-visit day care, and workplace day care).

認定こども園制度の改善 Improvement of the system for centers for early childhood education and care

認可・指導監督の一本化、学校及び児童福祉施設としての法的位置付けを持つ単一の施設である新たな「幼保連携型認定こども園」を創設する。

Establishment of centers for early childhood education and care (integrated center model), a new type of such centers. In this model, each center serves as a single facility that has the legal status of a school and a child welfare facility, under the integrated system of licensing, guidance and supervision.

子ども・子育て支援法
～認定こども園・幼稚園・保育所・小規模保育など共通の財政支援のための仕組み～
Children and Child-rearing Support Act
— Framework for the common financial support of centers for early childhood education and care, kindergartens, day care centers, local childcare, etc.

施設型給付 Institutional allowance

認定こども園 0～5歳
Centers for early childhood education and care allowance for children 0 to 5 years of age

幼保連携型 Integrated center model

○以下の制度改善を実施 ○ The following improvements are being made to the system:
- 認可・指導監督の一本化 Licensing, guidance, and supervision are being combined
- 学校及び児童福祉施設としての法的位置づけ These institutions are being legally established as schools and child welfare facilities.

幼稚園型	保育所型	地方裁量型
Kindergarten model	Day care center model	Local discretion model

幼稚園 3～5歳	保育所 0～5歳
Preschools for children 3 to 5 years of age	Day care centers for children 0 to 5 years of age
	※私立保育所については、児童福祉法第24条により市町村が保育の実施義務を担うことに基づく措置として、委託費を支弁
	Note: As for private day care centers, consignment fees are paid by municipalities based on their obligation to prove day care funds according to Article 24 of the Child Welfare Act.

地域型保育給付 Local childcare allowance

家庭的保育、小規模保育、居宅訪問型保育、事業所内保育
Home-based day care, small-sized day care, home-visit day care, and workplace day care

---

保育に関する認可制度の改善 Improvement of the day care licensing system

認可制度を前提としながら、大都市部の保育需要の増大に機動的に対応できるよう、客観的な認可基準に適合する場合は、欠格事由に該当する場合や供給過剰による需給調整が必要な場合を除き、認可するものとする。

With the premise of a licensing system, day care providers shall be licensed if they comply with objective licensing standards in order to quickly respond to the growing demand for day care in large urban areas, excluding those subject to ground for disqualification and when it is necessary to adjust supply and demand when there is an excess in the supply of day care services.

これらにより、質の高い学校教育・保育の総合的提供、保育の量的拡充、地域の子ども・子育て支援の充実が図られることが見込まれる。

As a result of these initiatives, unified provision of enhanced high-quality schooling and day care, expansion of childcare availability, and full support of local children and child-rearing can be expected.

4 児童手当制度について
The Child Allowance System

家庭等の生活の安定に寄与し、次代の社会を担う児童の健やかな成長に資する。

To contribute to a stable family lifestyle and play a part in the healthy growth of children who will be responsible for society in the next generation as adults.

概 要   Summary

(1) 支給対象
中学校修了まで(15歳の誕生日後の最初の3月31日まで)の児童を養育している者
(2) 支給額
①所得制限額未満である者
3歳未満　月15,000円
3歳以上小学校修了前(第1子、第2子)　月10,000円
3歳以上小学校修了前(第3子以降)　　月15,000円
中学生　月10,000円
②所得制限額以上である者
当分の間の特例給付　月5,000円
※所得制限額は、年収960万円(夫婦・児童2人世帯)を基準に設定
(3) 費用負担
国と地方(都道府県・市区町村)、事業主が費用を負担
令和2年度の給付総額2兆929億円(予算ベース)
(4) その他
①児童が日本国内に居住していることを要件とする(留学中の場合等を除く)。
②父母が離婚又は離婚協議中で別居している場合は、児童と同居しているものに支給する(単身赴任の場合を除く)。
③未成年後見人や父母指定者(父母等が国外にいる場合のみ)に対しても父母と同様の要件で支給する。
④児童養護施設に入所している児童等については、原則としてその施設の設置者等に支給する。
⑤保育料を手当から直接徴収できるようにしている。学校給食費等については、本人同意により手当から納付することができる仕組みとしている。

(1) Payment eligibility
For persons raising junior high school aged-children and younger (until March 31st following the child's 15th birthday)
(2) Amount of payment
1. Persons earning less than the income limit
Under age 3: 15,000 yen/month
From age 3 to completion of elementary school (1st and 2nd children): 10,000 yen/month
From age 3 to completion of elementary school (3rd child): 15,000 yen/month
Junior high school student: 10,000 yen/month
2. Persons earning more than the income limit
Special payment for the time being: 5,000 yen/month
(Income limit is 9,600,000 yen/year for a household with three dependents)
(3) Cost burden
The cost for child allowances will be assumed at the national level and by localities and business owners in accordance with the provisions of the Child Allowance Act.
Total disbursements for FY2020 are estimated at 2.0929 trillion yen. (budget basis)
(4) Other
① Children must be living within Japan (with the exception of instances in which they are living abroad on a foreign exchange).
② When parents are separated due to divorce or living separately during a divorce process, payments will be made to the person with whom the child is living.
③ Payments to guardians of minors and designated guardians (only when parents are living outside of Japan) will be made based on the same requirements as for parents.
④ The heads of the facilities will be paid for children residing in children's homes.
⑤ The system will make it possible to pay day care fees directly from the allowance. Also, a framework will be designed allowing parents to pay for school meals and similar expenses directly from the allowance if they so choose.

制度の沿革   History of System

昭和47年	児童手当制度発足。15歳までの第3子以降に月3,000円を支給(所得制限あり)
昭和57年	行政改革特例法による特例措置(所得制限の強化と特例給付の実施)
その後、制度改正	対象や金額の拡充、事業主拠出金の徴収開始など
平成18年度	0歳～小学校修了前の子どもを対象とする(所得制限あり)
～平成21年度	3歳未満　月10,000円
	3歳以上小学校修了前(第1子、第2子)　月5,000円
	3歳以上小学校修了前(第3子)　月10,000円
平成22年4月	「平成22年度等における子ども手当の支給に関する法律」
～平成23年9月	0歳～中学校修了前の子ども　月13,000円(一律)
平成23年10月～	「平成23年度における子ども手当の支給等に関する特別措置法」
平成24年4月～	改正児童手当法施行(所得制限導入は6月～)

1972:	Child allowance system established. Payment of 3,000 yen/month made for 3rd or later child through the age of 15 (with income restrictions).
1982:	Special measures based on administrative reform exception law (enhancement of restrictions and special exception allowances).
	System reforms thereafter: Expansion of eligibility and amounts, start of collection of contributions from business owners, etc.
FY2006~:	Children from age 0 through elementary school become eligible (with income restrictions)
~FY2009:	Children under age 3: 10,000 yen/month
	Age 3 through elementary school (1st and 2nd children) 5,000 yen/month
	Age 3 through elementary school (3rd child) 10,000 yen/month
April 2010	"FY2010 Child Allowance Act"
~Sept. 2011	Children from age 0 through middle school 13,000 yen/month (for all)
Oct. 2011~	"Act on Special Measures on Child Allowance Payments in FY2011"
April 2012	Enactment of the revised Child Allowance Act (with the new income limits introduced in June 2012)

5 地域子育て支援拠点事業
Community-based childrearing support center

地域子育て支援拠点事業とは、子育て中の親子が気軽に集い、相互交流や子育ての不安・悩みを相談できる場所で、全国に7,578か所設置されています（令和元年度）。公共施設や保育所、児童館等の地域の身近な場所で、乳幼児のいる子育て中の親子の交流や育児相談、情報提供等を実施します。NPOなど多様な主体の参画による地域の支え合い、子育て中の当事者による支え合いにより、地域の子育て力の向上を目指します。

Community-based childrearing support centers are places where parents and their children can comfortably gather and socialize and the parents can consult about their child-rearing concerns and worries. Childrearing support centers have been established in 7,578 locations nationwide(FY2019). Conveniently located at community sites such as public facilities, nursery schools and children's halls, the centers provide places for mothers engaged in childrearing and their infant children to come and socialize; they also offer consultation on childrearing, provide information, and more. Regional childrearing capabilities are to be improved through support by NPOs and various other organizations that participate in the centers, and also through the mutual support among parents engaged in childrearing. Support is also being promoted for such things as expanding the meeting places at centers and creating temporary meeting places when establishing permanent facilities is difficult.

地域子育て支援拠点事業の実施形態（一般型・連携型）
Form in which services are carried out for Community-based childrearing support center
(General Model and Collaborative Model)

形態 Form	一般型 General Model	連携型 Collaborative Model
機能 Function	常設の地域の子育て拠点を設け、地域の子育て支援機能の充実を図る取組を実施 With this type of base, a permanent site for gathering is established, and effort is made to provide a full range of regional child-rearing support functions.	児童館等の児童福祉施設等や多様な子育て支援に関する施設に親子が集う場を設け、子育て支援のための取組を実施 Space at child welfare facilities, such as Children's Halls, and other various child-rearing support related facilities is created for parents and their children to gather at, and efforts are made to provide child-rearing support.
実施主体 Organizations in charge	市町村（特別区を含む。）（社会福祉法人、NPO法人、民間事業者等への委託等も可） Municipalities (including special districts) (Operations may also be contracted out to social welfare corporations, NPOs, private companies, etc.)	
基本事業 Basic services	①子育て親子の交流の場の提供と交流の促進　②子育て等に関する相談・援助の実施 ③地域の子育て関連情報の提供　④子育て及び子育て支援に関する講習等の実施 (1) Providing a place for parents and their children to socialize, and promoting socializing　(2) Providing consultation and support for child-rearing (3) Providing regional information about child-rearing　(4) Conducting training related to child-rearing and to supporting child-rearing	
実施形態 Form in which the services are carried out	①～④の事業を子育て親子が集い、うち解けた雰囲気の中で語り合い、相互に交流を図る常設の場を設けて実施 ・地域の子育て拠点として地域の子育て支援活動の展開を図るための取組（加算） 　一時預かり事業や放課後児童クラブなど多様な子育て支援活動を拠点施設で一体的に実施し、関係機関等とネットワーク化を図り、よりきめ細かな支援を実施 ・出張ひろばの実施（加算） 　常設の拠点施設を開設している主体が、週1～2回、1日5時間以上、親子が集う場を常設することが困難な地域に出向き、出張ひろばを開設 ・地域支援の取組の実施（加算）※ 　①地域の多様な世代との連携を継続的に実施する取組 　②地域の団体と協働して伝統文化や習慣・行事を実施し、親子の育ちを継続的に支援する取組 　③地域ボランティアの育成、町内会、子育てサークルとの協働による地域団体の活性化等地域の子育て資源の発掘・育成を継続的に行う取組 　④家庭に対して訪問支援等を行うことで地域とのつながりを継続的に持たせる取組 　※利用者支援事業を併せて実施する場合は加算しない。 ・配慮が必要な子育て家庭等への支援（加算） 　配慮が必要な子育て家庭等の状況に対応した交流の場の提供等ができるよう、専門的な知識等を有する職員の配置等を実施 ・研修代替職員配置（加算） 　職員が研修に参加した際、代替職員を配置	①～④の事業を児童館等の児童福祉施設等で従事する職員等のバックアップを受けて効率的かつ効果的に実施 ・地域の子育て力を高める取組の実施（加算） 　拠点施設における中・高校生や大学生等ボランティアの日常的な受入・養成の実施 ・配慮が必要な子育て家庭等への支援（加算） 　配慮が必要な子育て家庭等の状況に対応した交流の場の提供等ができるよう、専門的な知識等を有する職員の配置等を実施 ・研修代替職員配置（加算） 　職員が研修に参加した際、代替職員を配置
従事者 Staff	子育て支援に関して意欲があり、子育てに関する知識・経験を有する者（2名以上） People (at least 2) who are highly motivated to provide child-rearing support and have knowledge and experience in child-rearing. Day care teachers, etc. (at least 2 people)	子育て支援に関して意欲があり、子育てに関する知識・経験を有する者（1名以上）に児童福祉施設等の職員が協力して実施 Individuals (at least 1) who are highly motivated to provide child-rearing support and have knowledge as well as experience in child-rearing work together with employees from child welfare facilities and similar institutions.
実施場所 Sites used for bases	公共施設空きスペース、商店街空き店舗、民家、マンション・アパートの一室、保育所、幼稚園、認定こども園等を活用 Empty space at community facilities, vacant stores in shopping districts, units in condominium buildings or apartment houses, day care centers, kindergartens, centers for early childhood education and care.	児童館等の児童福祉施設等 Child Welfare Facilities and similar locations, such as Children's Halls.
開設日数等 Number of days of operation	週3～4日、週5日、週6～7日 / 1日5時間以上 3-4 days, 5 days or 6-7 days per week At least 5 hours per day	週3～4日、週5～7日 / 1日3時間以上 3-4 days or 5-7 days per week At least 3 hours per day

6 ファミリー・サポート・センター事業
Family Support Center Services

ファミリー・サポート・センター事業は、乳幼児や小学生等の児童を有する子育て中の労働者や主婦等を会員として、児童の預かり等の援助を受けたい人と援助を行いたい人との相互援助活動に関する連絡、調整等を行う事業です。令和元年度は931市区町村で実施されています。

Family support centers, whose members include child-rearing workers and wives with infants or elementary-school-aged children, provide communication and coordination regarding mutual support activities between persons seeking assistance, such as persons to watch over their children, and persons desiring to provide assistance. Participating municipalities are 931 in FY2019.

援助を受けたい会員：約60万人
援助を行いたい会員：約15万人

Members seeking assistance:about 600 thousand
Members desiring to provide assistance:about 150 thousand

7 育児休業
Childcare Leave

①育児・介護休業法
The Child Care and Family Care Leave Act

育児・介護休業法では、職業生活と家庭生活の両立を図るため、労働者が育児休業、介護休業、子の看護休暇、介護休暇を取得できることを労働者の権利として規定し、短時間勤務などを始めとした育児又は家族の介護を行う労働者等を支援する措置を講ずることを、事業主に義務付けています。

In order to enable compatibility between work life and family life, the Child Care and Family Care Leave Act provides workers with rights to obtain childcare leave, family care leave, and child nursing leave, short term family care leave, and obligates business owners to take measures, such as shortening of work hours, to support workers engaged in child-rearing or family care.

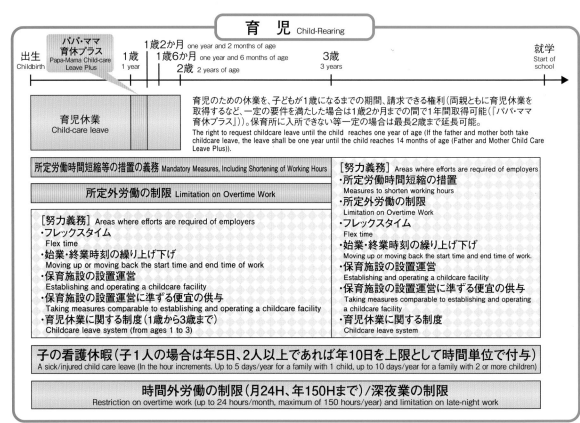

②育児休業取得率の推移 Change in the Rate at Which Child-care Leave Is Taken

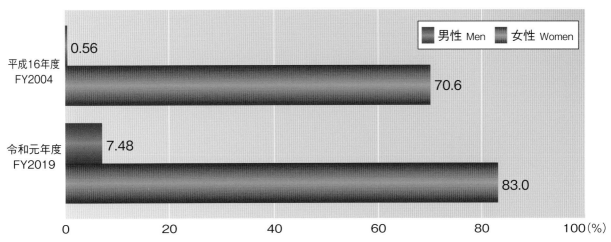

男性 Men　女性 Women

平成16年度 FY2004: 0.56 / 70.6
令和元年度 FY2019: 7.48 / 83.0

0　20　40　60　80　100(%)

厚生労働省「女性雇用管理基本調査」(平成16年度)
「雇用均等基本調査」(令和元年度)

目標値 Target values
男性の育児休業取得率 Rate at which men take child-care leave

2.63%（2011年度） ➡ 10%（2017年度）※「子ども・子育てビジョン」参考指標 ➡ 13%（2020年度）※雇用戦略対話 ➡ 30%（2025年度）※少子化社会対策大綱

育児休業取得率＝
Rate at which child-care leave is taken

出産者のうち、調査時点までに育児休業を開始した者
（開始予定の申出をしている者を含む。）の数
The number of people, among those who gave birth in the fiscal year studied in the survey,
who began child-care leave during that year (Includes those who applied to begin child-care leave.)

―――――――――――――――――――――

調査前年度1年間の出産者
（男性の場合は配偶者が出産した者）の数
The total number of people who gave birth in the fiscal year studied in the survey
(includes the number of male employees' wives who gave birth)

---

③第1子出生年別にみた、第1子出産前後の妻の就業変化
Changes in employment of wives before and after birth of first child by year in which first child was born

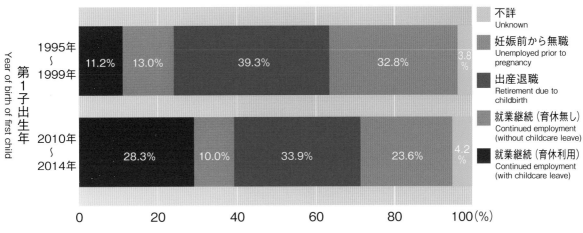

第1子出生年 Year of birth of first child

1995年～1999年: 11.2% / 13.0% / 39.3% / 32.8% / 3.8%
2010年～2014年: 28.3% / 10.0% / 33.9% / 23.6% / 4.2%

0　20　40　60　80　100(%)

不詳 Unknown
妊娠前から無職 Unemployed prior to pregnancy
出産退職 Retirement due to childbirth
就業継続（育休無し）Continued employment (without childcare leave)
就業継続（育休利用）Continued employment (with childcare leave)

国立社会保障・人口問題研究所「第15回出生動向基本調査」

2. 母子保健の施策
Maternal and Child Health (MCH)

わが国の母子保健施策は、母子保健法・児童福祉法等に基づき行われています。母子保健活動は、広く母性を対象とした母性保健施策と乳幼児に対する保健施策とを一貫した体系のもとに行うこととされています。

Policies and measures for mother and child health in Japan are based on Maternal and Child Health Law, Child Welfare Law, etc. Activities for mother and child health have been implemented under the stream-lined system of integrating health measures for maternity and babies.

1 母子保健施策のしくみ
Organization of MCH Services

学校保健、児童福祉に関する対策 Policies for School Health and Child Welfare

連携 Linked ⇕　　　　　連携 Linked ⇕

市町村 Municipalities

- 母子健康手帳の交付 Issuance of Maternal and Child Health Handbook
- 保健指導 Health Guidance
- 訪問指導 妊産婦、新生児、未熟児 Home visit to pregnant mothers, newborns and premature babies
- 未熟児養育医療の給付 Health care benefits for premature babies
- 健康診査 妊産婦、乳幼児、1歳6か月児、3歳児 Health check-ups for expectant mothers, newborns, 18-months-olds, 3-yr-olds

基本的母子保健サービスの実施
Provision of Basic Mother and Child Health Service

技術的援助
Technical Support

都道府県 Prefectures

- 療育の給付 Long-term Health care

専門的母子保健サービスの実施
Implementation of Specialized Mother-Child Health Services

市町村保健センターなどの整備、保健師などの人材の確保・養成、母子保健地域組織の育成
Establishment of municipal health centers etc., hiring and training of health professionals, development of regional mother-child health organizations

母子保健対策の基盤整備
Promotion of health maintenance for mothers and babies

国および都道府県 医療施設の整備 National and Prefectural levels: Construction of health care facilities

国 調査研究 National level: Investigation/Research

母性、乳幼児の健康の保持増進 Basic services of Mother-child health measure

2 「健やか親子21（第2次）」（母子保健の国民運動計画（平成27年度～令和6年度））の推進
Promotion of "Healthy Parents and Children 21 (Second Phase)" (Maternal and Child Health National Movement Plan (2015-2024))

○関係者が一体となって推進する母子保健の国民運動計画
A plan for a national movement on maternal and child health promoted through unified efforts by different stakeholders

○21世紀の母子保健の取組の方向性と目標や指標を示したもの
Providing directions, goals and guidelines on maternal and child health programs in the 21ST century

○第1次計画（平成13年～平成26年）・第2次計画（平成27年度～令和6年度）
The first round: 2001-2014, the second round: 2015-2024

健やか親子21

「すべての子どもが健やかに育つ社会」の実現 Building "A Society for Healthy Development of All Children"

【基盤課題A】 Fundamental issue A	【基盤課題B】 Fundamental issue B	【基盤課題C】 Fundamental issue C	【重点課題①】 Priority #1	【重点課題②】 Priority #2
切れ目ない妊産婦・乳幼児への保健対策 Seamless public health for pregnant women and infants	学童期・思春期から成人期に向けた保健対策 Public health from school age, adolescence to adulthood	子どもの健やかな成長を見守り育む地域づくり Developing supportive communities for children's healthy development	育てにくさを感じる親に寄り添う支援 Empathic support for parents with difficulties in child-rearing	妊娠期からの児童虐待防止対策 Child abuse prevention starting from pregnancy

企業 Companies
医療機関 Healthcare facilities
研究機関 Research Institutes
学校 Schools
NPO
住民（親子）Residents (parents and children)
連携と協働 Collaboration and cooperation
地方公共団体 Local governments
健やか親子21推進協議会 Healthy Parents and Children 21 Promotion Council
モニタリングの構築 Building a monitoring system
国（厚生労働省、文部科学省等）
National Governments (Ministry of Health, Labour and Welfare; Ministry of Education, Culture, Sports, Science and Technology; etc.)

①乳児死亡率の国際比較
（出生1,000対）

Infant mortality rate :
International comparison
（per 1,000 live birth）

$$乳児死亡率 = \frac{1歳未満の死亡数}{出　生　数} \times 1,000$$

$$Infant\ mortality\ rate = \frac{No.\ of\ deaths\ under\ 1year\ of\ age}{No.\ of\ live\ births} \times 1,000$$

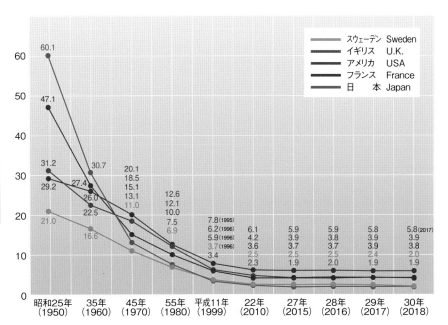

②妊産婦死亡率の国際比較
（出生10万対）

Maternal mortality rate :
International comparison
（per 100,000 live birth）

$$妊産婦死亡率 = \frac{妊産婦死亡数}{出　産　数} \times 10万$$

$$Maternal\ mortality\ rate = \frac{No.\ of\ maternal\ deaths}{No.\ of\ live\ births} \times 100,000$$

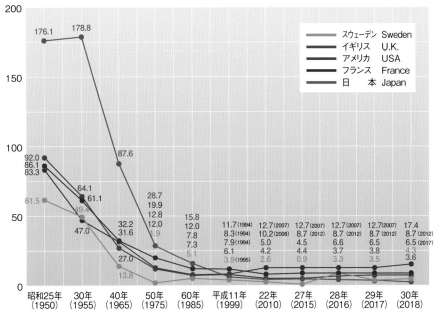

③周産期死亡率の国際比較
（出生1,000対）

Perinatal mortality rate :
International comparison
（per 1,000 live births）

$$周産期死亡率 = \frac{妊娠期28週以後の死産数 + 生後1週未満の新生児の死亡数}{出　生　数} \times 1,000$$

$$Perinatal\ mortality\ rate = \frac{No.\ of\ fetal\ deaths\ of\ 28\ weeks\ or\ more\ of\ pregnancy + No.\ of\ deaths\ under\ 1week\ of\ age}{No.\ of\ live\ births} \times 1,000$$

平成23年まではOECD「Health Data」、平成24年以降はOECD「Health Statistics」

1 認可保育所
Licensed Day Care Centers

「認可保育所」は、一定の基準に則り都道府県知事等が認可した保育所で、児童福祉施設の設備及び運営に関する基準を遵守し、保育所保育指針に基づく保育を行う児童福祉施設です。また、認可保育所の保育は、養護と教育を一体的に行うことをその特性としています。

"Licensed day care centers" are day care centers that have been approved by prefectural governors in accordance with specific criteria. They observe minimum standards on facilities and operation, and provide care based on care guidelines. Licensed day care centers also have the characteristic of providing centralized care and education.

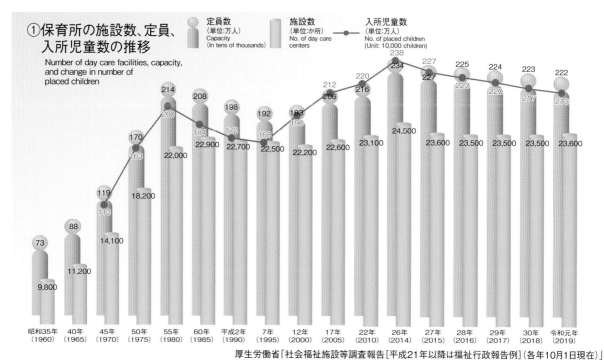

①保育所の施設数、定員、入所児童数の推移
Number of day care facilities, capacity, and change in number of placed children

凡例:
定員数（単位:万人） Capacity (In tens of thousands）
施設数（単位:か所） No. of day care centers
入所児童数（単位:万人） No. of placed children (Unit: 10,000 children)

	昭和35年(1960)	40年(1965)	45年(1970)	50年(1975)	55年(1980)	60年(1985)	平成2年(1990)	7年(1995)	12年(2000)	17年(2005)	22年(2010)	26年(2014)	27年(2015)	28年(2016)	29年(2017)	30年(2018)	令和元年(2019)
定員数	73	88	119	170	214	208	198	192	193	212	220	238	227	225	224	223	222
入所児童数			113	163	200	184	172	168	190	206	216	234	227	223	220	217	213
施設数	9,800	11,200	14,100	18,200	22,000	22,900	22,700	22,500	22,200	22,600	23,100	24,500	23,600	23,500	23,500	23,500	23,600

厚生労働省「社会福祉施設等調査報告[平成21年以降は福祉行政報告例]（各年10月1日現在)」

②認可保育所の年齢階層別入所児童の推移
Trends in ratios of children in licensed day care centers by age

凡例:
0歳児 0-year-old
1、2歳児 1,2-year-old
3歳児 3-year-old
4歳以上児 4 and over

0歳児	1、2歳児	3歳児	4歳以上児	年
0.3%	7.1%	13.2%	79.4%	昭和45年 113万人 1970 (In tens of thousands)
0.9%	14.0%	19.4%	65.7%	昭和55年 200万人 1980 (In tens of thousands)
1.4%	16.2%	18.4%	64.0%	平成2年 172万人 1990 (In tens of thousands)
2.1%	22.2%	19.0%	56.7%	平成12年 190万人 2000 (In tens of thousands)
7.4%	31.0%	20.6%	41.0%	平成22年 220万人 2010 (In tens of thousands)
8.0%	32.3%	20.0%	39.7%	平成26年 238万人 2014 (In tens of thousands)
7.9%	32.6%	19.9%	39.6%	平成27年 227万人 2015 (In tens of thousands)
8.0%	32.8%	19.8%	39.4%	平成28年 223万人 2016 (In tens of thousands)
8.0%	33.2%	19.8%	39.0%	平成29年 220万人 2017 (In tens of thousands)
8.0%	33.5%	19.7%	38.8%	平成30年 217万人 2018 (In tens of thousands)
7.8%	33.4%	19.8%	38.7%	令和元年 213万人 2019 (In tens of thousands)

厚生労働省「社会福祉施設等調査報告[平成22年以降は福祉行政報告例]（各年10月1日現在)」

③待機児童数の推移
Change in the Number of Children on Enrollment Waiting Lists

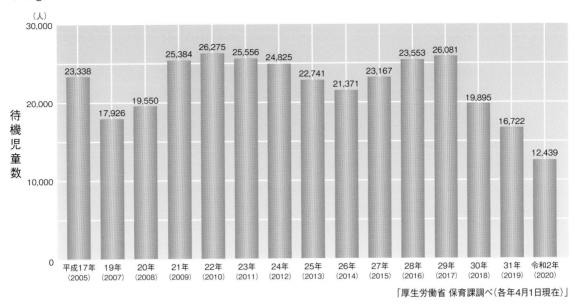

「厚生労働省 保育課調べ（各年4月1日現在）」

④認可保育所を中心とした多様な保育
Diverse childcare services—Focusing on those offered at licensed day care centers

事業名 Program name	事業内容 Program Contents	実施ヶ所数 No. of locations providing service
一時預かり Temporary placement	子育て家庭における保護者の休養・急病や育児疲れ解消等に対応するため、子どもを一時的に預かり保育すること。 Childcare that involves taking in a child on a temporary basis in order to provide a child-rearing guardian rest or recovery from illness or exhaustion stemming from child-rearing duties.	9,967ヶ所 （平成30年度） 9,967 locations (FY2018)
延長保育 Extended childcare	保護者の就労形態の多様化、通勤時間の増加等により通常保育時間では間に合わない事態に対応するため、朝・晩に時間を延長して保育を行うこと。 Extended childcare provided in morning or evening hours in order to cope with diversified working arrangements or increasing working hours on the part of the guardian.	28,476ヶ所 （平成30年度） 28,476 locations (FY2018)
夜間保育 Evening childcare	夜間において保育を実施すること。 Childcare provided during the evening.	79ヶ所 （平成31年度） 79 locations (FY2019)
病児保育 Sick child day care	子どもが病気の際に自宅での保育が困難な場合、病気の児童を一時的に保育すること。 Temporary childcare provided to children with illnesses in cases where due to a child's illness care at home is not feasible.	3,130ヶ所 （平成30年度） 3,130 locations (FY2018)

（注）実施ヶ所数については、認可保育所以外の施設で実施する場合も含む。
Note: The number of locations providing childcare services also includes facilities other than licensed day care centers.

2 認定こども園
Center for Early Childhood Education and Care

「認定こども園」とは教育・保育を一体的に行う施設で、幼稚園と保育所の両方の良さを併せ持っている施設です。

以下の機能を備え、職員配置や保育内容等の基準を満たす施設は、都道府県等から認可又は認定を受けることができます。

①就学前の子どもを、保護者が働いている、いないにかかわらず受け入れて、幼児教育及び保育を一体的に行う機能

②子育て相談や、親子の集いの場の提供等、地域における子育て支援を行う機能

Centers for early childhood education and care are the facilities that provide education and care in an integrated manner, having advantages of both kindergartens and day care centers.

They can be licensed or certified by prefectures and other authorities if they have the following functions and meet the requirements on staff and care.

(1) Having functions to accept preschool children, regardless of the employment status of their parents, and to provide them with early childhood education and care in an integrated manner.

(2) Serving as facilities that provide consultation on child-rearing, places for parents and children to gather, and community-based support on child-rearing.

| 都道府県及び指定都市、中核市 Prefectures, designated cities and core cities | 認可 Licensing → | 幼保連携型認定こども園 (学校かつ児童福祉施設) Center for early childhood education and care (integrated center model)(school and child welfare facility) **幼保連携型認定こども園** Integrated center model | 幼稚園的機能と保育所的機能の両方の機能を併せ持つ単一の施設として、認定こども園としての機能を果たすタイプ A single facility with functions of both a kindergarten and a day care center serving as a center for early childhood education and care. |

都道府県及び指定都市、中核市 Prefectures, designated cities and core cities

認定 Certifying →
幼稚園 (学校) Kindergarten (school) ／ 保育所機能 Functions of a day care center
幼稚園型認定こども園 Kindergarten model

認可幼稚園が、保育を必要とする子どものための保育時間を確保するなど、保育所的な機能を備えて認定こども園としての機能を果たすタイプ
A licensed kindergarten serving as a center for early childhood education and care by having functions of a day care center, such as ensuring time to provide services for children who need day care.

認定 Certifying →
幼稚園機能 Functions of a kindergarten ／ 保育所 (児童福祉施設) Day care center (child welfare facility)
保育所型認定こども園 Day care center model

認可保育所が、保育を必要とする子ども以外の子どもも受け入れるなど、幼稚園的な機能を備えることで認定こども園としての機能を果たすタイプ
A licensed day care center serving as a center for early childhood education and care by having functions of a kindergarten, such as accepting children who may not need day care.

認定 Certifying →
幼稚園機能 ＋ 保育所機能 (認可外保育施設等) Functions of a kindergarten + functions of a day care center (non-licensed day care facility, etc.)
地方裁量型認定こども園 Local discretion model

認可保育所以外の保育機能施設等が、保育を必要とする子ども以外の子どもも受け入れるなど、幼稚園的な機能を備えることで認定こども園の機能を果たすタイプ
A day care facility other than a licensed day care center serving as a center for early childhood education and care by having functions of a kindergarten, such as accepting children who may not need day care.

厚生労働省資料

認定こども園認定状況 The Situation Regarding Certification of Centers for Early Childhood Education and Care

認定件数 Number of certifications	(内訳) (Details)			
	幼保連携型 Collaboration of kindergarten and day care center model	幼稚園型 Kindergarten model	保育所型 Day care center model	地方裁量型 Local discretion model
8,016	5,688	1,200	1,053	75

「内閣府 子ども・子育て本部(令和2年4月1日現在)」

3 企業主導型保育事業
Company-led Childcare Business

企業主導型の事業所内保育事業を主軸として、多様な就労形態に対応する保育サービスの拡大を行い、保育所待機児童の解消を図り、仕事と子育てとの両立に資することを目的として、企業主導型保育事業を実施しています。
○多様な就労形態に対応した保育サービスの拡大を支援するための仕組みであること
○地域枠も自由に設定できること（利用定員の50％以内）
○運営費や施設整備については、子ども・子育て支援新制度の小規模保育事業等の公定価格に準じた支援が行われることなど、企業主導型保育事業の特色・メリットを活かした事業展開を図ることができます。

Company-led childcare businesses are provided, mainly through workplace day care programs led by companies, with aims to expand childcare services that accommodate various working arrangements, to address the problem with children on the waiting list for a day care center, and to help parents strike a balance between work and child-rearing.
These businesses can be developed while leveraging their unique characteristics and advantages.
○They should provide a mechanism to help expansion of childcare services that accommodate various working arrangements.
○They can freely make the services available to local residents (up to 50% of the total capacity).
○Regarding their costs for operation and maintenance, support should be provided according to official prices for small-sized day care under the comprehensive support system for children and child-rearing.

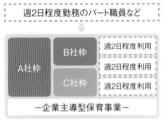

週2日程度就労など、多様な就業形態に対応した保育サービス

Childcare services to accommodate various working arrangements (e.g., working around 2 days/week)

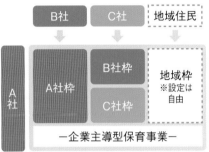

多様な就労形態に対応した延長保育、夜間保育、休日保育等多様な預かりを必要に応じて実施

Providing a variety of childcare services (e.g., extended hours, evening and holidays), as needed, to accommodate various working arrangements

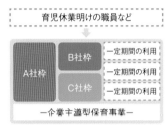

地域の保育所等に入所するまでの間など、必要とする期間に応じた柔軟な受け入れ
→継続就業を促進

Flexible periods of services according to needs (e.g., until the person starts using a local day care center)
→ Promoting continuous employment

内閣府 作成

4 認可外保育施設
Non-licensed Day Care Facilities

認可外保育施設は、保育を行うことを目的とした施設であって、認可を受けていない施設をいい、原則として事業開始から1か月以内に自治体への届出が必要です。運営主体は様々で、企業、NPO法人、個人などで、自治体等からの補助金を受けて運営されているところもあります。

Non-licensed day care facilities refer to the ones that aim to provide childcare without license. In principle, these facilities must notify the local government within one month of the commencement of their business. These childcare facilities are operated by various entities, including corporations, NPOs, and individuals, and some also operate with subsidies from local government and other sources.

○全国の認可外保育施設数と入所児童数の推移
Change in number of non-licensed day care facilities and number of placed children nationwide

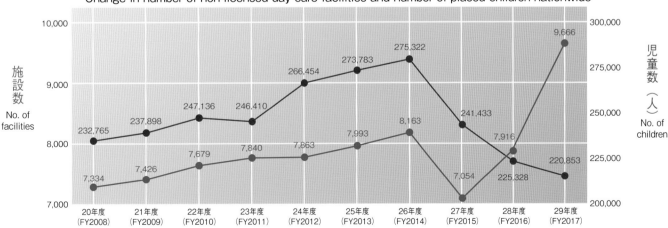

※子ども・子育て支援新制度が施行した平成27年度以降は、入所児童数に小学校就学児を除く。
* FY2015 (enforcement of the comprehensive support system for children and child-rearing)- : The number of placed children excludes elementary school children.

「厚生労働省 子ども家庭局総務課少子化総合対策室調べ」

4. 子どもが健やかに育つための施策
Measures for Enabling Children to Grow Up Healthy

すべての児童をより健やかに育成するための施策を児童健全育成施策とよんでいます。児童厚生施設のほか、地域を基盤として母親たちが児童健全育成活動を行う地域組織活動（母親クラブ数1,036、会員数38,324人／令和元年10月1日現在）、放課後児童クラブの設置運営、児童委員・主任児童委員（児童委員数228,206人。うち主任児童委員数21,117人／令和元年12月1日現在）による子どもの見守り・相談・援助、児童福祉文化財の普及などを行っています。

Measures for enabling all children to grow up healthier are referred to as measures for the promotion of children's health. In addition to facilities for the betterment of children's lives, there are regional organization activities carried out by mothers for promoting children's health (1,036 mother's clubs with 38,324 members as of October 1st, 2019), the establishment and management of after-school children's clubs, and commissioned child welfare volunteers as well as commissioned child welfare volunteer directors (228,206 commissioned child welfare volunteers with 21,117 commissioned child welfare volunteer directors as of December 1st,2019) that look after children, offer consultations, provide support, and spread cultural assets for children's welfare.

1 児童厚生施設数の推移
Change in Number of Facilities for Betterment of Children's Life

児童に健全な遊びを与えて、その健康を増進し、又は情操をゆたかにすることを目的とする施設で、児童館・児童センター、児童遊園 を指します。

Facilities for the betterment of children's lives: facilities designed to provide children with healthy playtime, improve children's health, and promote healthy emotional development. These include children's halls, children's centers, and children's playgrounds.

児童館・児童遊園数の推移
Changes in no. of Children's Halls and Children's Playgrounds.

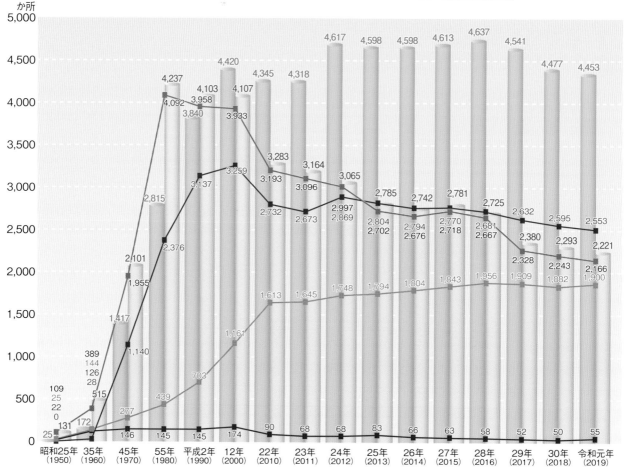

厚生労働省「社会福祉施設等調査」

2 放課後児童健全育成事業
After-school Child Sound Upbringing Services

①放課後児童クラブ数及び登録児童数の推移（各年5月1日現在）
Changes in no. of After-School Children's Clubs and registered children.（As of May 1, each year）

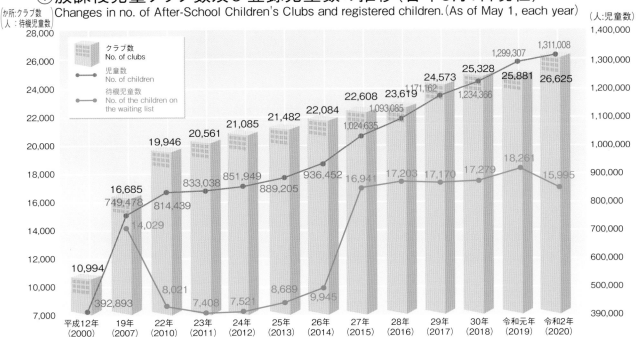

(注)平成23年は東日本大震災の影響によって調査を実施できなかった岩手県及び福島県の12市町村を除いた数値。
(Note) In 2011, due to the impact of the Great East Japan Earthquake, figures exclude 12 municipalities of Iwate prefecture and Fukushima prefecture in which the survey could not be conducted.

厚生労働省「放課後児童健全育成事業（放課後児童クラブ）の実施状況」

②放課後児童クラブの実施状況（令和2年5月1日現在）
State of After-School Children's Clubs.（As of May 1, 2020）

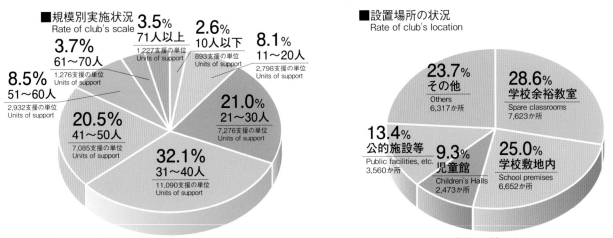

(注)「支援の単位」とは、「放課後児童健全育成事業の設備及び運営に関する基準」により、児童の集団の規模を示す新たな基準として導入したもの。
Note: "Units of support" has been introduced as the new standard to indicate the scale of children's groups based on "The Standards Concerning Facilities and Management of an After-school Children's Clubs".

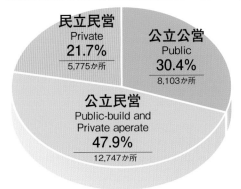

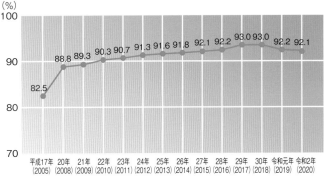

厚生労働省「放課後児童健全育成事業（放課後児童クラブ）の実施状況」

(注)平成23年は東日本大震災の影響によって調査を実施できなかった岩手県及び福島県の12市町村を除いた数値。
(Note) In 2011, due to the impact of the Great East Japan Earthquake, figures exclude 12 municipalities of Iwate prefecture and Fukushima prefecture in which the survey could not be conducted.

目で見る児童福祉2021　*33*

何らかの事情により家庭での養育が困難又は受けられなくなった児童、社会環境・親子関係や対人関係等の不調から情緒障害や非行を起こす児童に対する福祉として、児童相談所等による相談と指導および里親委託、児童福祉施設への入所・通所措置などの施策が行われています。

Measures such as consultations and guidance provided by children's guidance centers, admission/institutionalization of children at child welfare facilities, and entrustment of children to foster parents are implemented to support the welfare of children from families which have difficulty raising or cannot raise children due to various factors, and children who are emotionally-disturbed or delinquent due to factors such as their social environment, relationship with parents, or relationships with others.

1 里親制度
Foster Care System

①里親制度 Foster Care System

平成28年度の児童福祉法改正により、里親委託を原則とすることが明確にされ、里親制度のさらなる推進を図っています。

We are promoting a foster care system that was regarded as a principle by the revision of the Child Welfare Law in 2016.

種類 Type of foster care	養育里親 Care-providing foster parents	専門里親 Specialized foster parents	養子縁組を希望する里親 Foster parents wishing to adopt	親族里親 Kindred foster parents
対象児童 Eligible children	要保護児童(保護者のいない児童又は保護者に監護させることが不適切であると認められる児童) Children requiring protective care (children who do not have legal guardians or children whose legal guardians have been judged unfit to care for them)	要保護児童のうち都道府県知事等が特に必要と認めたもの ①児童虐待等の行為により心身に有害な影響を受けた児童 ②非行等の問題を有する児童 ③身体障害、知的障害又は精神障害がある児童 Children whom prefectural governors, etc., have judged to be particularly needy of protective care (1) Children who have suffered emotional and physical injury due to acts of child abuse, etc. (2) Children who have problems with juvenile delinquency, etc. (3) Children who have a physical, mental or emotional disability	要保護児童(保護者のいない児童又は保護者に監護させることが不適切であると認められる児童) Children requiring protective care (children who do not have legal guardians or children whose legal guardians have been judged unfit to care for them)	次の要件に該当する要保護児童 ①当該親族里親に扶養義務のある児童 ②児童の両親その他当該児童を現に監護するものが死亡、行方不明、拘禁等の状態となったことによりこれらのものにより養育が期待できないこと。 Children requiring protective care who meet the following requirements (1) The child's kindred foster parents have the duty to support the child. (2) The child's parents or other people who should take care of the child are deceased, missing, incarcerated, or in some other situation such that they cannot be expected to care for the child.

②登録里親数等の推移 Change in the Number of Registered Foster Parents, etc.

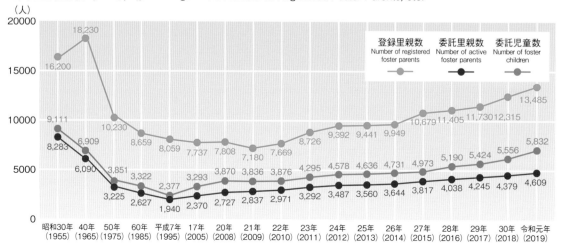

（注）平成22年の福島県分については、厚生労働省家庭福祉課調べ
(Note) Fukushima prefecture data for 2010 is based on the home welfare findings of the Ministry of Health, Labour and Welfare.

厚生労働省「福祉行政報告例」

③里親委託児童の年齢構成比 Age composition of children entrusted to foster parents

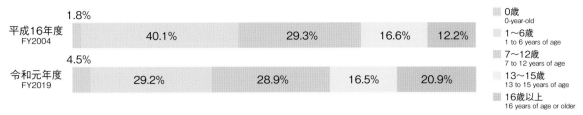

平成16年度
FY2004: 1.8% / 40.1% / 29.3% / 16.6% / 12.2%

令和元年度
FY2019: 4.5% / 29.2% / 28.9% / 16.5% / 20.9%

■ 0歳
0-year-old
□ 1〜6歳
1 to 6 years of age
■ 7〜12歳
7 to 12 years of age
■ 13〜15歳
13 to 15 years of age
■ 16歳以上
16 years of age or older

厚生労働省「福祉行政報告例」

2 要保護児童施設の枠組み
Framework for Facilities for Children Requiring Protective Care

①養護ニーズのある子ども・家庭への施策のしくみ
The Mechanism of Measures for Children Who require Protective Care and for Their Families

養護ニーズのある子ども・家庭（父母の死亡、離別、病気、虐待、棄児、養育困難等）
Children who require protective care, and their families
(parents who are deceased, divorced, ill, abusive, have abandoned their children, have difficulty in raising their children, etc.)

 相談
Consultation

 相談、通報等
Consultation, notification, etc.

地域での支援
Community support

市町村における
子育て家庭への様々な支援
Various supports for families
raising children by municipalities, towns and villages

児童家庭支援センター
Child and family support
centers

相談、協力、通報等
Consultation, cooperation,
notification, etc.

相談、協力等
Consultation, cooperation,
etc.

児童相談所
子どもの一時保護、委託・入所措置、
治療、自立へ向けた支援等
Child guidance centers
Temporary care, institutionalization/entrustment,
medical treatment, support for becoming
independent

家庭の代わりに子どもを養育する施設等
Facilities that raise children in place of their families

より家庭的な養育環境 A more family-like child-rearing environment

児童養護施設
Children's
nursing home
605か所
605 locations

乳児院
Infant homes
140か所
140 locations

小規模グループケア
本園
ユニットケア（分園型）
1,790か所
Small-scale group care
(Unit care in the main
facility)
(Branch model)
1,790 locations

地域小規模
児童養護施設
（グループホーム）
423か所
Community small-scale
child-protection
institutions
(group homes)
423 locations

小規模住居型
児童養育事業
（ファミリーホーム）
372か所
Small-scale businesses
that give children a
homelike upbringing
(family homes)
372 locations

里親
Foster parents
登録里親 12,315世帯
委託里親 4,379世帯
Number of Registered
Foster Parents: 12,315
Number of Active Foster
Parents: 4,379

自立援助ホーム 176か所
Homes supporting independence 176 locations

養護ニーズの解消、自立、家庭復帰（家族再統合）
Elimination of need for protective care, Independence, Return to home (reintegration of family)

参考:「社会的養育の推進に向けて（令和2年10月）」

②児童養護施設入所児童の入所理由の変化
Trends in causes for placement into childrens homes

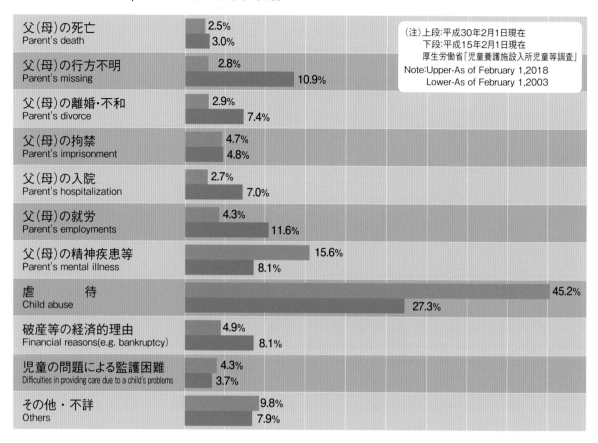

	上段	下段
父（母）の死亡 Parent's death	2.5%	3.0%
父（母）の行方不明 Parent's missing	2.8%	10.9%
父（母）の離婚・不和 Parent's divorce	2.9%	7.4%
父（母）の拘禁 Parent's imprisonment	4.7%	4.8%
父（母）の入院 Parent's hospitalization	2.7%	7.0%
父（母）の就労 Parent's employments	4.3%	11.6%
父（母）の精神疾患等 Parent's mental illness	15.6%	8.1%
虐待 Child abuse	45.2%	27.3%
破産等の経済的理由 Financial reasons(e.g. bankruptcy)	4.9%	8.1%
児童の問題による監護困難 Difficulties in providing care due to a child's problems	4.3%	3.7%
その他・不詳 Others	9.8%	7.9%

(注)上段:平成30年2月1日現在
下段:平成15年2月1日現在
厚生労働省「児童養護施設入所児童等調査」
Note:Upper-As of February 1,2018
Lower-As of February 1,2003

③児童養護施設入所児童の年齢構成比
Age-specific ratio to the admitted children in Children's Homes

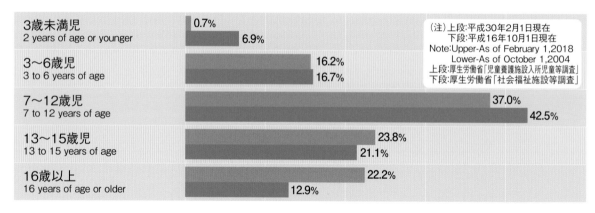

	上段	下段
3歳未満児 2 years of age or younger	0.7%	6.9%
3〜6歳児 3 to 6 years of age	16.2%	16.7%
7〜12歳児 7 to 12 years of age	37.0%	42.5%
13〜15歳児 13 to 15 years of age	23.8%	21.1%
16歳以上 16 years of age or older	22.2%	12.9%

(注)上段:平成30年2月1日現在
下段:平成16年10月1日現在
Note:Upper-As of February 1,2018
Lower-As of October 1,2004
上段:厚生労働省「児童養護施設入所児童等調査」
下段:厚生労働省「社会福祉施設等調査」

④児童心理治療施設入所児童の年齢構成比
Ratio of Accommodated in short-term Treatment Facility for Children with Emotional Disturbance by age

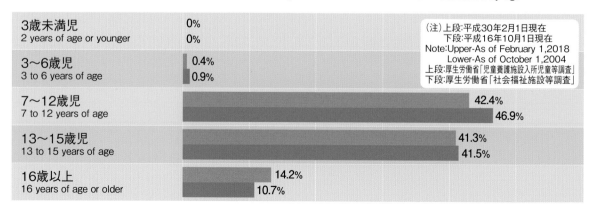

	上段	下段
3歳未満児 2 years of age or younger	0%	0%
3〜6歳児 3 to 6 years of age	0.4%	0.9%
7〜12歳児 7 to 12 years of age	42.4%	46.9%
13〜15歳児 13 to 15 years of age	41.3%	41.5%
16歳以上 16 years of age or older	14.2%	10.7%

(注)上段:平成30年2月1日現在
下段:平成16年10月1日現在
Note:Upper-As of February 1,2018
Lower-As of October 1,2004
上段:厚生労働省「児童養護施設入所児童等調査」
下段:厚生労働省「社会福祉施設等調査」

3 児童虐待への対応
Addressing Child Abuse

児童虐待に関する相談対応件数は年々増加しており、子どもの生命が奪われる重大な事件も後を絶たないなど、深刻な状況が続いています。児童虐待防止対策の強化を図るため、令和元年6月に成立した改正児童福祉法等に基づき、保護者等による体罰の禁止、児童福祉司等の増員や児童相談所の設置基準の策定といった体制強化・設置促進、転居時の情報提供やDV対策との連携といった関係機関との連携強化などに取り組むこととしました。また、児童虐待問題への国民の理解の浸透及び児童虐待防止に向けた国民的意識の高揚・定着を図るため、民間団体、地方自治体等とともに、児童虐待防止のシンボルであるオレンジリボンを用いた取り組みを行っています。

子ども虐待防止のオレンジリボン

The number of consultations regarding child abuse is increasing year by year; the serious condition has been continuing, including a number of major cases where children's lives are taken away. Based on the amended Child Welfare Act (enacted in June 2019), various measures will be taken to step up efforts to prevent child abuse, including: prohibition of corporal punishment by guardians, system reinforcement and development (e.g., increase the number of child welfare officers, set criteria for establishment of child guidance centers), and better cooperation among relevant bodies (e.g., share information when residents have moved, cooperation with DV programs). In addition, programs are also being organized in collaboration with private organizations and local municipalities while using orange ribbons, which symbolize child abuse prevention, in order to promote public awareness of child abuse and its prevention.

① 地域における児童虐待防止のシステム
Community-based Child Abuse Prevention System

● 従来の児童虐待防止対策は、「児童相談所」のみで対応する仕組みであったが、平成16年の児童虐待防止法等の改正により、「市町村」も虐待通告の通告先となり、「市町村」「児童相談所」が二層構造で対応する仕組みとなっている。

Child Abuse Prevention measures used to be implemented by Child Guidance Center solely in the past, but since the revision of Child Abuse Prevention Law in 2004, municipalities also have been receiving notice of child abuse as well. Child Guidance Centers and municipalities have formed a two-layered response structure.

● 現在、各市町村単位で、要保護児童対策地域協議会及び市区町村子ども家庭総合支援拠点の設置が進められているところ（平成29年4月1日現在、要保護児童対策地域協議会は、99.7%が設置）。

Each city, town and village is currently establishing its own Regional Council for Children in Need of Protection and Comprehensive Support Center for Children and Families. (As of April 1, 2017, 99.7% of the municipalities had established Regional Council for Children in Need of Protection.)

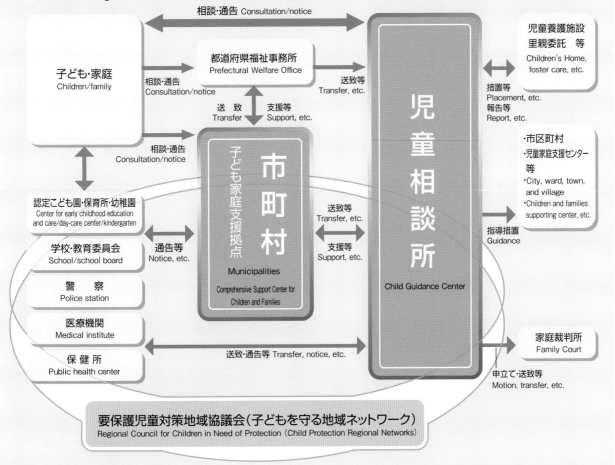

②児童相談所における児童虐待相談対応件数と、市町村における児童虐待相談対応件数の推移

Changes in number of child abuse consultations responses at child guidance centers and number of child abuse consultation responses at municipalities

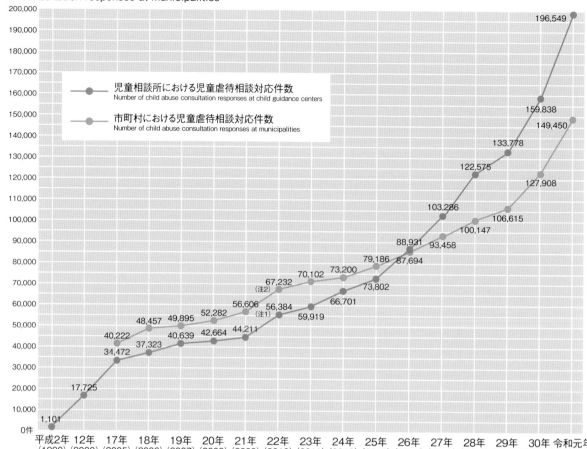

- 児童相談所における児童虐待相談対応件数
  Number of child abuse consultation responses at child guidance centers
- 市町村における児童虐待相談対応件数
  Number of child abuse consultation responses at municipalities

平成2年(1990) 1,101 / 12年(2000) 17,725 / 17年(2005) 34,472・40,222 / 18年(2006) 37,323・48,457 / 19年(2007) 40,639・49,895 / 20年(2008) 42,664・52,282 / 21年(2009) 44,211・56,606(注1) / 22年(2010) 56,384・67,232(注2) / 23年(2011) 59,919・70,102 / 24年(2012) 66,701・73,200 / 25年(2013) 73,802・79,186 / 26年(2014) 87,694・88,931 / 27年(2015) 93,458・103,286 / 28年(2016) 100,147・122,575 / 29年(2017) 106,615・133,778 / 30年(2018) 127,908・159,838 / 令和元年(2019) 149,450・196,549

(注1)東日本大震災の影響により、福島県を除いて集計した数値。
(Note 1) Due to the impact of the Great East Japan Earthquake, the figures were aggregated excluding Fukushima prefecture.
(注2)東日本大震災の影響により、岩手県、宮城県(仙台市を除く)の一部及び福島県を除いて集計した数値。
(Note 2) Due to the impact of the Great East Japan Earthquake, the figures were aggregated excluding Fukushima prefecture and parts of Iwate prefecture and Miyagi prefecture (Sendai City excluded).

厚生労働省「福祉行政報告例」

③児童相談所における児童虐待種類別割合グラフ／年齢別被虐待児数割合グラフ(令和元年)

Proportion graph by type of child abuse / proportion graph of abused children by age at child guidance centers (2019)

■児童虐待種類別
By type of child abuse

総数 193,780件
Total number: 193,780

■年齢別被虐待児数
Abused children by age

総数 193,780件
Total number: 193,780

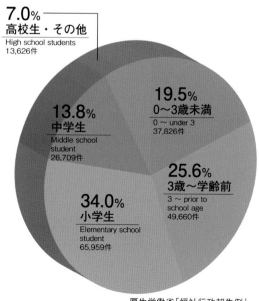

児童虐待種類別
- 1.1% 性的虐待 Sexual abuse 2,077件
- 25.4% 身体的虐待 Physical abuse 49,240件
- 56.3% 心理的虐待 Psychological abuse 109,118件
- 17.2% 保護の怠慢(ネグレクト) Failure to protect (Neglect) 33,345件

年齢別被虐待児数
- 7.0% 高校生・その他 High school students 13,626件
- 19.5% 0〜3歳未満 0 〜 under 3 37,826件
- 13.8% 中学生 Middle school student 26,709件
- 25.6% 3歳〜学齢前 3 〜 prior to school age 49,660件
- 34.0% 小学生 Elementary school student 65,959件

厚生労働省「福祉行政報告例」

④児童相談所における虐待相談受理後の対応内容
Response details following receipt of abuse consultation at child guidance centers

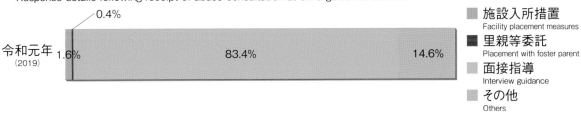

令和元年
(2019)

0.4%

1.6% | 83.4% | 14.6%

■ 施設入所措置
Facility placement measures

■ 里親等委託
Placement with foster parent

■ 面接指導
Interview guidance

■ その他
Others

厚生労働省「福祉行政報告例」

⑤要保護児童対策地域協議会（又は虐待防止ネットワーク）の設置数及び割合
Number and Percentage of Establishments of the Regional Council for Children in Need of Protection（Child Abuse Prevention Networks）

■要保護児童対策地域協議会（又は虐待防止ネットワーク）の設置数及び割合
Number and Percentage of Establishments of the Regional Council for Children in Need of Protection（Child Abuse Prevention Networks）

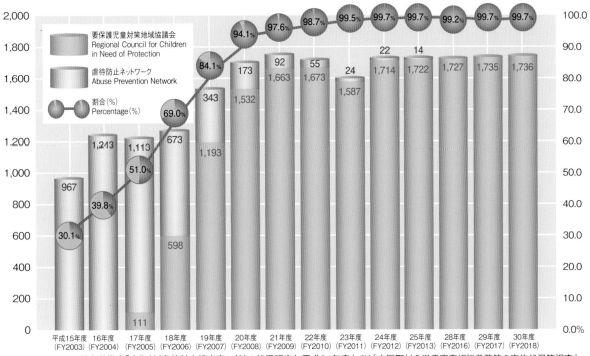

厚生労働省「市町村（虐待対応担当窓口等）の状況調査」、平成24年度までは「市区町村の児童家庭相談業務等の実施状況等調査」、
平成25年度は「子どもを守る地域ネットワーク等調査」

（注）平成17年度までは6月1日現在の調査であり、平成18年度からは4月1日現在の調査である。
　　　平成16年度まではネットワークの設置数であり、平成17年度からは地域協議会又はネットワークの設置数である。
　　　割合は、全市町村のうち地域協議会又はネットワークを設置している市町村の率を示す。
　　　平成23年度は東日本大震災の影響により、岩手県、宮城県、福島県を除いて集計した数値。
　　　平成28年度以降は虐待防止ネットワークを除した数値。

Note : Data as of June 1 (until fiscal 2005) and April 1 (from fiscal 2006). The number of Networks is shown until fiscal 2004, while the number of Regional Councils or Networks is shown from fiscal 2005. The percentage indicates the ratio of municipalities nationwide that have established a Regional Council or Network. Due to the Great East Japan Earthquake, values from Iwate, Miyagi, and Fukushima Prefectures are not included for fiscal 2011. The data from fiscal 2016 exclude Child Abuse Prevention Networks.

⑥乳児家庭全戸訪問事業実施状況／養育支援訪問事業実施状況（平成30年度）
House-call services for all households with babies / House-call services to support children (FY2018)

■乳児家庭全戸訪問事業実施状況（4月1日現在）
Current state of infant home visiting service for all houses (as of April 1)

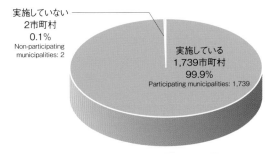

実施していない
2市町村
0.1%
Non-participating municipalities: 2

実施している
1,739市町村
99.9%
Participating municipalities: 1,739

■養育支援訪問事業実施状況（4月1日現在）
Current state of upbringing support visiting service (as of April 1)

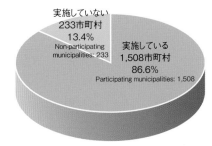

実施していない
233市町村
13.4%
Non-participating municipalities: 233

実施している
1,508市町村
86.6%
Participating municipalities: 1,508

厚生労働省「市町村（虐待対応担当窓口等）の状況調査」

6. ひとり親家庭への施策
Measures for Single-Parent Families

ひとり親家庭の親は、生計の維持と子どもの養育という二つの大きな責任をもっており、子どもを育てながら自立した生活を送ることができるように、子育て・生活支援、就業支援、養育費確保支援、経済的支援の4本柱により総合的な自立支援策を推進しています。

経済的支援の一つである児童扶養手当は、生別母子世帯等の18歳未満の児童を監護する母、監護しかつ生計を同じくする父、又は養育する者に支給されます。就労等の収入額と手当額を加えた年間総収入額がなだらかに増加するように手当額はきめ細かく設定され、また子どもが2人の場合は最大10,190円、3人目以降の場合は1人ごとに最大6,110円が加算されます。

Parents of single-parent families have two important responsibilities: the maintenance of livelihood and the raising of children. In order to enable such parents to live independently while raising their children, comprehensive independence support measures are being promoted based on the following four pillars: employment support, child-raising and lifestyle support, support for children, procurement of child-raising costs, and economic support.
One form of economic support, the child rearing allowance, is paid to single mothers, working fathers, or other persons caring for a child under age 18. The allowance is set precisely so that the annual combined work income and allowance increases gradually. Also, when there are two children, up to 10,190 yen is added; when there are three or more children, up to 6,110 yen for each child is added.

1 就業・自立に向けた総合的な支援策
Comprehensive Measures to Support Employment and Independence

○総合的な支援のための相談窓口の整備（就業支援専門員の配置推進）
Developing consultation services for comprehensive support (Promoting use of employment support specialists)

ひとり親家庭の支援に関する主な課題 Main issues regarding support for single-parent families

- ○相談支援体制が不十分（多岐にわたる課題を把握・整理し、適切な支援メニューにつなげることができていない）
- ○多くが非正規雇用で働いており、稼働所得が少ないため、個々の状況に応じた就業支援が必要

○Inadequate consultation and support systems (unable to understand/sort out various issues and link clients to appropriate support)
○Individualized employment support is needed since many parents have a non-regular and low-wage job

総合的な支援のための相談窓口の整備 Developing consultation services for comprehensive support

- ○支援メニューを組み合わせて総合的・包括的な支援を行うワンストップの相談窓口を設置し、必要とする家庭に必要とする支援が届くよう相談支援体制を構築（就業支援専門員の配置推進）
- ○ワンストップの相談窓口による関係機関と連携した就業支援を行い、安定した雇用による就労自立を実現

○Developing a support system so that families can receive necessary support by developing one-stop consultation desks that combine support menus and provide comprehensive support (Promoting use of employment support specialists)
○Obtaining a job and independence through stable employment by coordinated employment support from the "one-stop" service and relevant organizations

総合的な支援のための相談窓口の整備（市レベル）
Developing consultation services for comprehensive support (at City level)

母子・父子自立支援員
Support specialist for independence of single-parent families

＋

就業支援専門員
Employment support specialist

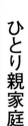

ひとり親家庭 Single-parent families

適切な支援メニューの組み合わせ
Combination of appropriate support menus

- ○自治体の規模、支援サービスの状況など地域の実情に応じた相談窓口のワンストップ化を推進
  Promoting development of "one-stop" consultation services tailored to each local community
- ○就業を軸とした的確な支援の提供
  Providing appropriate support centering on employment
- ○支援施策の広報啓発活動の実施
  PR activities on support measures

子育て・生活支援 Support in child-rearing and daily living

- ○母子・父子自立支援員による相談支援
- ○ヘルパー派遣、保育所等の優先入所
- ○子どもの生活・学習支援事業等による子どもへの支援
- ○母子生活支援施設の機能拡充　　など

○Counseling and support by support specialists for independence of single-parent families
○Priority access to helpers and nurseries
○Helping children through support programs for children in daily living and studying
○Enhancing the functions of maternal and child living support facilities

就業支援 Employment support

- ○母子・父子自立支援プログラムの策定やハローワーク等との連携による就業支援の推進
- ○母子家庭等就業・自立支援センター事業の推進
- ○能力開発等のための給付金の支給　　など

○Promoting employment support through the development of independence support programs for single-parent families and collaboration with public employment security offices
○Promoting the role of employment and independence support centers for single-parent families
○Providing benefits for skill development, etc.

養育費確保支援 Securing child support payments

- ○養育費相談支援センター事業の推進
- ○母子家庭等就業・自立支援センター等における養育費相談の推進
- ○「養育費の手引き」やリーフレットの配布　　など

○Promoting the role of consultation centers for child support payments
○Promoting consultation service on child support payments at places such as employment and independence support centers for single-parent families
○Distributing handbooks and leaflets on child support payments

経済的支援 Economic support

- ○児童扶養手当の支給
- ○母子父子寡婦福祉資金の貸付
  　就職のための技能習得や児童の修学など12種類の福祉資金を貸付　　など

○Providing child rearing allowances
○Providing welfare loans for single-parent families
　12 types of welfare loans (e.g., helping parents learn skills for employment and helping children learn)

2 母子・父子自立支援員による相談 (令和元年度)
Consultation by Support Specialist for Independence of Single-parent Families (fiscal 2019)

相談割合　% of cases consulted

| 生活一般 General consultation 28.3% | 経済的支援・生活援護 Consultation regarding financial support/welfare 58.6% |

児童
Consultation on children
10.0%

その他
Others
3.1%

3 児童扶養手当
Child Rearing Allowance (Aid to Dependent Children)

①児童扶養手当受給世帯数 (令和元年度)
No. of households granted Child Rearing Allowance (fiscal 2019)

総　数 Total	生別世帯 Lilfelong separation		死別世帯 Bereaved households	未婚の世帯 Single Parent	障害者世帯 Parent(s) with disability	遺 棄 世 帯 Desertion	その他の世帯 Others
	離婚 divorce	その他 others					
900,673	752,613	1,553	8,001	99,638	6,027	1,630	31,211

厚生労働省「福祉行政報告例 (令和元年度)」

(注)「生別世帯 その他」に「DV保護命令世帯」を含む。

②児童扶養手当の給付水準 [手当受給者と子ども1人の世帯]
Benefit level of child rearing allowance [Households with beneficiary(ies) and a child]

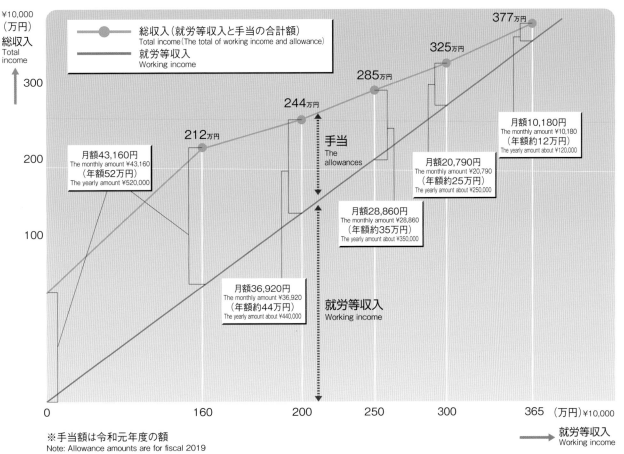

※手当額は令和元年度の額
Note: Allowance amounts are for fiscal 2019

7. 子どもの貧困に対する施策
Measures against Poverty among Children

平成25年に、貧困の状況にある子どもが健やかに育成される環境を整備するとともに、教育の機会均等を図るため、子どもの貧困対策を総合的に推進することを目的として「子どもの貧困対策の推進に関する法律」が制定されました。子どもの貧困対策は、子どもの現在及び将来がその生まれ育った環境によって左右されることのない社会を実現し、子育てや貧困を家庭のみの責任とするのではなく、地域や社会全体で課題を解決するという意識を強く持ち、子どものことを第一に考えた適切な支援を包括的かつ早期に講じるものとされました。

The Act on Promotion of Measures against Poverty among Children was enacted in 2013. It aims to promote comprehensive measures against poverty among children in order to build the environment that enables healthy development of children in poverty and to provide equal educational opportunities. We should build a society where present and future conditions of children do not depend on the environment they grow up in. Also, child-rearing and poverty are not just family responsibilities but the issues to be resolved by communities and the entire society. Strongly based on these viewpoints, the measures against poverty among children are set to provide appropriate support that puts children first in a comprehensive and prompt manner.

1 子供の貧困対策に関する大綱について（令和元年11月29日閣議決定）

目的・理念

○現在から将来にわたって、全ての子供たちが前向きな気持ちで夢や希望を持つことのできる社会の構築を目指す。
○子育てや貧困を家庭のみの責任とするのではなく、地域や社会全体で課題を解決するという意識を強く持ち、子供のことを第一に考えた適切な支援を包括的かつ早期に講じる。

基本的な方針

○親の妊娠・出産期から子供の社会的自立までの切れ目ない支援
○支援が届いていない、又は届きにくい子供・家庭への配慮
○地方公共団体による取組の充実
　　　　　　　　　　　　　　　　　など

子供の貧困に関する指標

○生活保護世帯に属する子供の高校・大学等進学率
○高等教育の修学支援新制度の利用者数
○食料又は衣服が買えない経験
○子供の貧困率
○ひとり親世帯の貧困率
　　　　　　　　　　　　など、39の指標

指標の改善に向けた重点施策

＜教育の支援＞
○幼児教育・保育の無償化の推進及び質の向上
○地域に開かれた子供の貧困対策のプラットフォームとしての学校指導・運営体制の構築
　・スクールソーシャルワーカーやスクールカウンセラーが機能する体制の構築、少人数指導や習熟度別指導、補習等のための指導体制の充実等を通じた学校教育による学力保障
○高等学校等における修学継続のための支援
　・高校中退の予防のための取組、高校中退後の支援
○大学等進学に対する教育機会の提供
○特に配慮を要する子供への支援
○教育費負担の軽減
○地域における学習支援等

＜保護者に対する職業生活の安定と向上に資するための就労の支援＞
○職業生活の安定と向上のための支援
　・所得向上策の推進、職業と家庭が安心して両立できる働き方の実現
○ひとり親に対する就労支援
○ふたり親世帯を含む困窮世帯等への就労支援

＜生活の安定に資するための支援＞
○親の妊娠・出産期、子供の乳幼児期における支援
　・特定妊婦等困難を抱えた女性の把握と支援 等
○保護者の生活支援
　・保護者の自立支援、保育等の確保 等
○子供の生活支援
○子供の就労支援
○住宅に関する支援
○児童養護施設退所者等に関する支援
　・家庭への復帰支援、退所等後の相談支援
○支援体制の強化

＜経済的支援＞
○児童手当・児童扶養手当制度の着実な実施
○養育費の確保の推進
○教育費負担の軽減

施策の推進体制等

＜子供の貧困に関する調査研究等＞
○子供の貧困の実態等を把握するための調査研究
○子供の貧困に関する指標に関する調査研究
○地方公共団体による実態把握の支援

＜施策の推進体制等＞
○国における推進体制
○地域における施策推進への支援
○官公民の連携・協働プロジェクトの推進、国民運動の展開
○施策の実施状況等の検証・評価
○大綱の見直し

General Principles Concerning Measures against Poverty among Children (approved in a Cabinet meeting on November 29, 2019)

Goals and Philosophy

○Aiming to build a society where all children can have dreams and hopes with positive feelings now and in the future.
○Providing appropriate support that puts children first in a comprehensive and prompt manner, with emphasis on the viewpoint that child-rearing and poverty are not just family responsibilities but the issues to be resolved by communities and the entire society.

Key principles

○Providing seamless support from a parent's pregnancy and childbirth to a child's independence in society
○Taking consideration for children/families who have not been reached or those who are hard to reach
○Enhancing initiatives by local governments, etc.

Indicators on poverty among children

○Proportion of children on public assistance who go to high school, college, etc.
○Number of people who use the new tuition support system for higher education
○Inability to buy food or clothing
○Child poverty rate
○Poverty rate among single-parent households and others
(39 indicators in total)

Priority measures to improve the indicators

<Educational support>
○Promoting the efforts to make preschool education and childcare free and improving their quality
○Building school guidance and management systems as platforms for measures against child poverty which are open to communities
・Guaranteeing academic abilities by school education through such initiatives as: development of systems where school social workers and school counselors can function, small-group guidance, group education based on students' abilities, and enhancement of teaching systems for remedial classes
○Supporting students to continue their education at high school, etc.
・Preventing high school dropout and supporting those who have dropped out of high school
○Providing opportunities for college and other higher education
○Supporting children who require special care
○Easing the financial burden on education
○Providing academic support, etc. in communities

<Support to help stabilize the livelihood>
○Support during pregnancy, childbirth and infancy
・Grasping the situation of and supporting the women who have difficulty, including "specified expectant mothers"
○Livelihood support for parents
・Supporting parents' independence, securing childcare, etc.
○Livelihood support for children
○Employment support for children
○Support on housing
○Support on those who have left children's homes, etc.
・Supporting them to return to their families and providing consultation after they leave the homes
○Enhancement of support systems

<Employment support for parents to help stabilize and improve their work>
○Support for more stable and better work
・Promoting measures to increase income and realizing work styles that support work-life balance
○Employment support for single parents
○Employment support for households in need, including two-parent households

<Financial support>
○Steadily implementing child allowance and child support allowance systems
○Promoting measures to secure child support payments
○Easing the financial burden on education

Systems to promote the measures

<Research on poverty among children>
○Research to understand the current state of poverty among children, etc.
○Research on indicators of poverty among children
○Support for local governments' efforts to understand the current state

<Systems to promote the measures>
○Promotion systems at the national level
○Supporting the promotion of measures at the local level
○Promoting collaborative and joint projects by public and private sectors, and developing a national movement
○Examining and evaluating the implementation of the measures, etc.
○Reviewing the General Principles

2 相対的貧困率の推移について
Trends in Relative Poverty Rates

相対的貧困率の年次推移
Trends in relative poverty rates

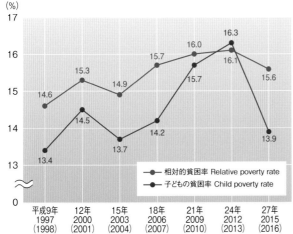

子どもがいる現役世帯（世帯主が18歳以上65歳未満）の世帯員の相対的貧困率
Relative poverty rates among working-age households with a child (heads of households are aged 18-64)

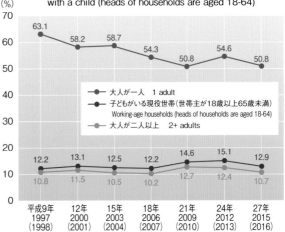

資料:「平成28年国民生活基礎調査」

8.障害児への施策
Services for Children with Disabilities

国連の児童権利宣言や児童の権利に関する条約にもあるように、子どもは心身ともに健全に育つ権利を保障されるべきもので、これは、障害のある子どもについても同様です。障害児に対する支援は、児童福祉法を基本として国、地方自治体等が相互に連携を図りながら児童福祉の向上に努めてきました。また、児童福祉法の改正により、平成24年4月から身近な地域で支援を受けられるよう従来の障害種別に分かれた施設体系を再編し、通所による支援を「障害児通所支援」に、入所による支援を「障害児入所支援」にそれぞれ一元化するとともに、障害児通所支援に係る実施主体については、都道府県から市町村に移行しました。併せて、学齢期における支援の充実のための「放課後等デイサービス」と、保育所などを訪問し専門的な支援を行うための「保育所等訪問支援」を創設するなど、支援体制の充実を図っています。

・知的障害とは、知的機能の障害が発達期（おおむね18歳まで）にあらわれ、日常生活に持続的な支障が生じているため、何らかの特別な援助を必要とする状態にあることをいいます。

・身体障害とは先天的あるいは後天的な理由で、身体機能の一部に障害を生じている状態にあることをいいます。
　身体障害児とは、手足の不自由な児童（肢体不自由児）、目の不自由な児童（視覚障害児）、耳の不自由な児童（聴覚障害児）など、からだの不自由な児童をいいます。

・発達障害とは、自閉症、アスペルガー症候群等の広汎性発達障害、学習障害、注意欠陥多動性障害などの脳機能の障害で、その症状が通常低年齢において発現するものをいいます。

As stated in the United Nations' Declaration of Rights of the Child and Convention on the Rights of the Child, the right of children to grow healthily in both body and mind should be assured and the same holds true for children with disabilities. Support for children with disabilities is based on the Child Welfare Act, and the national and local governments have worked together by coordinating to improve child welfare. Moreover, under the revised Child Welfare Act, several changes were made in April 2012 so that children could receive support in nearby communities. For example, while facilities under the old system were divided according to type of disabilities, they are consolidated under the new system, consisting of the following 2 services: "Day care for children with disabilities" where children go to the facility and "Institutional care for children with disabilities" where children live. Moreover, the administrative bodies responsible for day care were transferred from prefectures to local municipalities. Other new measures also started to enhance the support system, including "after-school day care services" to enhance support for school-aged children and "visiting support at nurseries" in which professionals visit nurseries to provide specialized support.

・An intellectual disability refers to a disability of intellectual function appearing during the developmental years (approximately up to age 18), which because of the occurrence of a continuous obstacle to daily life, requires some kind of special support.

・A physical disability refers to the occurrence of a disability to some physical functions due to congenital or acquired causes.
　Children with physical disabilities include those with physical, visual, and/or hearing impairments.

・Developmental disorder refers to pervasive developmental disorders including autism and Asperger syndrome, or a disability of mental capacity, such as a learning disability or attention-deficit/hyperactivity disorder, the symptoms of which usually are discovered at an early age.

障害児の状況
Current State of Children with Disabilities

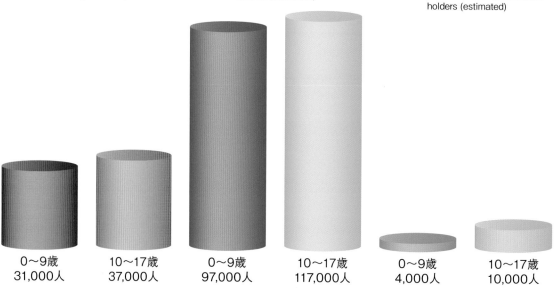

身体障害者手帳所持者数（推計値）
Number of physical disability certificate holders (estimated)

療育手帳所持者数（推計値）
Number of rehabilitation certificate holders (estimated)

精神障害者保健福祉手帳所持者数（推計値）
Number of mental disability certificate holders (estimated)

| 0〜9歳 31,000人 | 10〜17歳 37,000人 | 0〜9歳 97,000人 | 10〜17歳 117,000人 | 0〜9歳 4,000人 | 10〜17歳 10,000人 |

※鳥取県倉吉市は鳥取県中部地震の影響により、調査を実施していない。

厚生労働省「平成28年生活のしづらさなどに関する調査」（全国在宅障害児・者等実態調査）

2 障害児へのサービス内容及び支援体制例
Examples of Services and Support Systems for Children with Disabilities

支援の目標（例）
Support objectives (example)

| 親子関係、日常生活、遊び、集団等を通した発達の基礎づくり（心身、対人、言葉、ADL等）
Building of a foundation for development through parent-child relationships, daily life, play, groups, etc. (Body and mind, interpersonal, language, ADL, etc.) | 様々な生活体験を通じた生きる力に結びつく基礎的・基本的な知識・技能の習得（教科、買物や料理等／ADL、対人、余暇等）
Acquisition of foundational and basic knowledge and skills that lead to the power to live through various daily life experiences (School coursework, shopping and cooking, etc. / ADL, interpersonal, leisure, etc.) | 就労、地域生活につなげる支援（実習、自活訓練等）
Support that leads to employment and community life (Practical training, self-support training, etc.) |

【都道府県】
役割:高度の専門的支援・人材育成等
【Prefectures】
Role: high-level specialized support, human resource development, etc.

- 児童相談所・発達障害者支援センター等
Child guidance centers, support centers for persons with developmental disabilities, etc.
- 総合センター(医療機関、障害児入所施設、児童発達支援センター等の複合)
General centers (composition of medical institutions, Residential care facilities for children with disabilities, child development support centers etc.)
- 都道府県が設置する教育センター等
Education centers, etc. established by prefectures

【障害保健福祉圏域】
役割:専門的支援・地域支援等
【Areas of health and welfare for persons with disabilities】
Role: specialized support, local support, etc.

- 保健所・障害児等療育支援事業等
Health centers and care services for disabled children, etc.
- 障害児入所施設
Residential care facilities for children with disabilities
- 児童発達支援センター(医療型を含む)
Child development support centers (including medical)
- 放課後等デイサービス
Afterschool day services
- 特別支援学校(盲ろう養護学校・幼稚部を含む)、高等学校
Special support schools (including schools and special support schools for blind, deaf and disabled), high schools

【市町村】
役割:身近な地域で早い段階からの支援
【Municipalities】
Role: early-stage support in close-by areas

- 障害児相談支援／特定障害者相談支援・保健センター・家庭児童相談室等
Consultation and support on children with disabilities / support and health centers for persons with specific disabilities, and family and child consultation rooms, etc.
- 児童発達支援事業
Child development support programs
- 放課後等デイサービス
Afterschool day services
- 児童発達支援以外のサービス事業所(日中一時支援事業・訪問系サービス等(医療的ケアの実施を含む))
Service offices other than for child development support (daytime temporary support programs and visitation services, etc. (including provision of medical care))
- 保育所等訪問支援など
Day care centers, etc. visitation support, etc

役割:生活の場での支援
Role: support at living locations

一般子ども施策の施設
General children's facilities

- 子育て支援サービス
Child-rearing support services
- 放課後児童健全育成事業
Afterschool child healthy upbringing measures
- 保育所・幼稚園・認定こども園
Day care center, kindergarten, licensed center for early childhood education and care
- 学校(小中学校(特別支援学級))
Schools (elementary and middle schools (special support classes))

0 1 2 3 4 5 6 7 8 9 10 11 12 13 14 15 16 17 18 (歳) Age

3 障害児に関する手当制度の概要
Outline of Allowance Systems Related to Children with Disabilities

	特別児童扶養手当 Special Child Rearing Allowance	障害児福祉手当 Welfare Allowance for Children with Disabilities
目的 Objective	精神又は身体に障害を有する児童について手当を支給することにより、これらの児童の福祉の増進を図る。 To improve welfare of children with mental or physical disabilities by providing the allowance to them.	重度障害児に対して、その障害のため必要となる精神的、物質的な特別の負担の軽減の一助として手当を支給することにより重度障害児の福祉の向上を図る。 To improve welfare of children with severe disabilities by providing the allowance to them to partially cover the costs necessary to provide emotional and material support.
支給要件 Support Requirements	1.20歳未満　2.在宅のみ　3.父母又は養育者が受給 1. Under age 20 2. At-home only 3. The parent/guardian shall receive the support	1.20歳未満　2.在宅のみ　3.本人が受給 1. Under age 20 2. At-home only 3. Person in question receives the aid
障害程度 Degree of Disability ※右記は概ねの目安であり、基本的には、各手当の診断書に基き判定が行われる。	1級…身障1級2級及び3級の一部 2級…身障2級の一部、3級及び4級の一部 ※精神及び知的は上記と同程度 Level 1- part of physical disability levels 1, 2, and 3 Level 2- part of physical disability level 2, part of levels 3 and 4 * Mental/Intellectual disabilities are as above	身障の1級及び2級の一部 ※精神及び知的は上記と同程度 Physical disability level 1 and part of level 2 * Mental/Intellectual disabilities are as above
給付月額（令和2年度） Monthly Amount (2020)	1級52,500円　2級34,970円 Level 1 52,500 Yen Level 2 34,970 Yen	14,880円 14,880 Yen
所得制限（年収） Income Restriction (Annual Income)	1.本人（4人世帯）7,707千円　2.扶養（6人世帯）9,542千円 1. Person in question (4-person household) 7,707,000 Yen 2. Dependent (6-person household) 9,542,000 Yen	1.本人（2人世帯）5,656千円　2.扶養（6人世帯）9,542千円 1. Person in question (2-person household) 5,656,000 Yen 2. Dependents (6-person household) 9,542,000 Yen
給付人員（令和元年度末） No. of recepients (end of 2019)	1級95,555人　2級168,792人 Level 1 95,555 Level 2 168,792	63,584人 63,584
令和2年度予算額 FY2020 Budget Amount	132,828,249千円 132,828,249 thousand Yen	8,526,520千円 8,526,520 thousand Yen
負担率 Share	国10/10 National 10/10	国3/4　都道府県、市又は福祉事務所設置町村1/4 3/4 will be paid by the national government, 1/4 will be paid by prefectures, cities, or municipalities with welfare offices
支給事務 Procurement Affairs	国 National	都道府県、市又は福祉事務所設置町村 Conducted by prefectures, cities and municipalities with welfare offices.

（注）所得制限限度額は、平成14年8月からの額である。　Note: The income restriction amount is the amount effective since August 2002

4 発達障害児の概要
Overview of People with Developmental Disorders

●言葉の発達の遅れ
●コミュニケーションの障害
●対人関係・社会性の障害
●パターン化した行動、こだわり
● Delay in language development
● Communication difficulties
● Difficulties with interpersonal relationships and socialization
● Pattern behavior and obsessiveness

それぞれの障害の特性
Characteristics of the Disorders

知的な遅れを伴うこともあります
Mental retardation is sometimes involved.

注意欠陥多動性障害（AD/HD）
AD/HD(Attention-Deficit/Hyperactivity Disorder)
●不注意（集中できない）
●多動・多弁（じっとしていられない）
●衝動的に行動する（考えるよりも先に動く）
● Inattention (Can't concentrate.)
● Hyperactivity and talkativeness (Can't stay still.)
● Impulsiveness (Acts before thinking.)

自閉症
Autism

広汎性発達障害
PDD (pervasive developmental disorders)

アスペルガー症候群
Asperger syndrome

学習障害（LD）
LD (Learning Disorders)
●「読む」、「書く」、「計算する」等の能力が、全体的な知的発達に比べて極端に苦手
● Reading, writing, calculating, and other abilities are extremely poor as compared to the overall intellectual development.

●基本的に、言葉の発達の遅れはない
●コミュニケーションの障害
●対人関係・社会性の障害
●パターン化した行動、興味・関心のかたより
●不器用（言語発達に比べて）
● Basically, there is no delay in language development.
● Communication difficulties
● Difficulties with interpersonal relationships and socialization
● Pattern behavior and excessive focusing on particular interests and enthusiasms
● Clumsiness (as compared to language development)

※このほか、トゥレット症候群や吃音（症）なども発達障害に含まれます。
Tourette's syndrome and stuttering are also included in developmental disorders.

［参考］東日本大震災の被害状況
[Reference] Great East Japan Earthquake Damage Situation

①東日本大震災での被災者数
Number of victims from the Great East Japan Earthquake

死亡数 Number of fatalities	行方不明数 Number of missing	両親が死亡又は行方不明となった児童数 （ひとり親家庭であって、今回の震災によりそのひとり親が死亡又は行方不明となった児童を含む） Number of children whose parents are dead or missing (Including single-parent families in which as a result of the disaster, the parent of the child is either dead or missing)	ひとり親となった児童数 Number of children with single-parent
15,899人	2,527人	243人	1,548人
令和2年12月10日現在 警察庁まとめ Compiled by the National Police Agency as of December 10, 2020		平成30年3月1日現在 厚生労働省まとめ Compiled by the Ministry of Health, Labour and Welfare as of March 1, 2018	

②児童福祉施設の被害状況
Damage situation of child welfare facilities

	被害を受けた施設の数（全壊・半壊・一部損壊含む） Number of facilities suffering damage (including fully collapsed, half collapsed and partially damaged)
児童福祉施設数全体 Total number of child welfare facilities	745
うち認可保育所 Of which are licensed day care centers	672
うち社会的養護の施設 Of which are social care facilities	46
うち障害児関連施設 Of which are facilities related to disabled children	27

平成23年5月13日現在 厚生労働省まとめ